INSIDE OUT and Upside Down

HOW INTIMACY WITH JESUS CHANGES EVERYTHING

A SEVEN-WEEK BIBLE STUDY
WITH WEEKEND DEVOTIONS

JENNIFER HAYES YATES

Interior images and author photo by Genesis Shalom Harrington

Edited by Josiah Lee Yates

Formatting by Jen Henderson of Wild Words Formatting

jenniferhyates.com

Inside Out and Upside Down:
How Intimacy with Jesus Changes Everything

A 7-week Bible study with weekend devotions

Jennifer Hayes Yates

Download the *Inside Out Scripture Memory Cards* FREE!

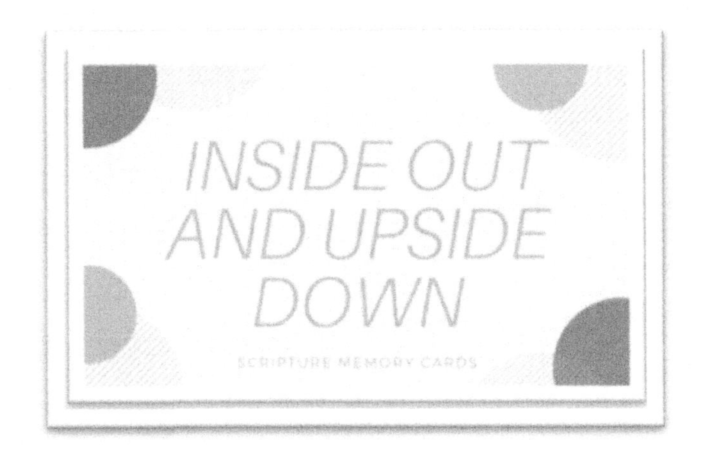

Just to say thanks, I want to give you my
Inside Out Scripture Memory Cards totally FREE!

To get the Scripture memory cards, enter this in your browser:

https://www.subscribepage.com/scripturecards

Table of Contents

PART 1

INSIDE OUT:

Religion vs. Relationship

Inside Out: Religion vs. Relationship

Do you ever wonder why some women seem so in love with Jesus that they just glow, and you love to be around them? They know the Word so well that they always have it on their lips. These are the ladies who are eager to pray with you when you have a need.

Others go to church, but never seem to be happy. They may even serve in the church, attend Sunday school, and be very faithful, but never seem to be fulfilled. They have a form of godliness about them, but seem to lack the power of God at work in their lives.

How can the same God be the object of worship for all of them, yet only a handful seem to be really changed by Him? If God is so powerful, why do many women still feel empty and confused? Why do so many give up and walk away from the church?

That second woman was me. I was in the church, serving God, yet still unsatisfied in so many areas of my life. I knew there was more than what I was experiencing. I wanted to be the Spirit-filled woman in love with Jesus. But at times, I just wanted to walk away from church altogether.

All that changed when I started getting to really know God.

My heart's desire is to see all women of God set free from bondage to sin, self, and society, and fall in love with the Savior. I'm not talking about going to church and being religious. I'm talking about knowing Jesus intimately and following Him with love and passion. I'm talking about a relationship with God that transcends culture and builds a Kingdom.

How did this passion develop for me?—through intimacy with God. And that's what I want for you. Some of you already have a personal relationship with Jesus. If that is the case, then my prayer is that God would use this study to draw you deeper into the things of God. Some of you are saved, but you don't understand what it means to know Jesus intimately. I pray this study would show you how.

And some of you don't even know why you are reading this right now. That's okay, too. My prayer for you is that in the pages of this book and the Scriptures you will read, you will discover a love that you have never known.

Jesus is real.

But He didn't die for you to get religion. I know that there are those who don't like it when I say that. I get it. Yes, the word religion is in the Bible. It's not so much the denotation (dictionary definition) that I have a problem with. It's the connotation (perceived understanding) of the word today.

> Religion: the belief in a god or in a group of gods
>
> an organized system of beliefs, ceremonies, and rules used to worship a god or a group of gods
>
> an interest, a belief, or an activity that is very important to a person or group[i]

The word religion itself is amoral—neither good nor bad. But just as Satan perverts many amoral concepts (such as money), he has perverted religion to blind people to its dangers. As you can see, the definition of religion applies to any religion, not just Christianity. So what makes Christianity different from every other religion? Why can't we just decide we are a Christian, go to a Christian church, and be okay with a "system of beliefs, ceremonies, and rules"?

That's what this Bible study is all about. Christianity is under fire right now all over the globe. We need to know the truth about God and not just what is culturally acceptable. There is one true God, and His name is Jesus Christ. He is the only way to heaven. But what He desires is to know you and be in a personal relationship with you. No other religion offers that.

If you are tired of trying to make life work on your own, this study is for you. If you know there is more to life than what you are personally experiencing, this study is for you. If you want more of the life and Spirit of Jesus bringing victory and passion to your life, this study is for you. If you are confused and don't even understand what it means to have a relationship with Jesus or how that could be possible, this study is for you.

So if you are ready, I invite you to dive in with me. Pray that the Holy Spirit will open your eyes and guide you into the truth that will set you free.

I'm already praying that for you.

WEEK 1

God's Desire for Relationship

**“O LORD,
YOU HAVE
SEARCHED
ME AND YOU
KNOW ME.”**

PSALM 139:1

1.1—EDEN: THE CHOICE TO SIN

I can remember when I was filling out my college application; the form had a box to check for religion. I wasn't saved at the time or even in church, but I checked the box for Christian. Why? Because I really thought that since I lived in America and I wasn't a Muslim, Buddhist, or Hindu, that basically made me a Christian.

I want to use this first week of study to help us understand that God's desire for us is to know Him and be in relationship with Him. So many people seem to think that as Americans, we are Christians by default. Or at least that once we go to church and do the outward religious expectations, we are okay with God and on our way to heaven. Nothing could be further from the truth.

The truth is that God has desired to know us and for us to know Him from the very beginning.

Let's begin today's lesson by looking at the Gospel of John. Read John 1:1-18.

Who was with God in the beginning?

What happened when He came into the world?

Why do you think the world He created did not recognize Him as God?

a. He didn't look like a god.

b. He didn't obey the Law.

c. He didn't go to church.

d. They didn't know God.

I want us to read the first three chapters of Genesis today to establish God's desire for relationship. I know that's a good bit of reading on the first day, but please bear with me. We can't really establish a good foundation without it. Please read Genesis chapter one. Who was with God at creation? (hint: 1:2)

We see the concept of the Trinity from the very beginning and the Words of John—God the Father, Son, and Holy Spirit are all three present at Creation.

Please read Genesis chapter two.

Why do you think God created Adam and Eve with the ability to think, reason, and make choices?

Now read Genesis chapter three.

What was God doing in 3:8?

What do you think it would be like to literally walk with God in a garden?

Does it sound to you like they had a relationship with God prior to sin coming into their lives?

In the first three chapters of Genesis (with a little help from John) we see God as Father, Son, and Holy Spirit. We see Him creating man and woman with a free will and the ability to think, reason, and choose between right and wrong. God gave Adam and Eve dominion over all the earth. God spoke freely with them and walked with them in the garden.

God created people because He wanted to. He made us in His image. He gave us free will because He wants us to choose to love Him. He desires a personal relationship with each of us.

Sin, however, has marred that relationship with God. God is holy. As a result of their sin, Adam and Eve were cast out of the garden and away from the tree of life, which would allow them to live forever. God did not make that choice; they did when they broke the one rule He gave them.

So God chose to make a way to redeem mankind back to Himself. He created them for fellowship. They chose sin. He created them to worship Him. They chose to listen to the lies of the enemy. He created them to love and live forever with Him. They chose to disobey His loving guidelines.

We all have an inborn desire to worship God, because that is what we were created for.

Haven't we, too? We all have an inborn desire to worship God, because that is what we were created for. We all have a desire to love and to be loved. But we choose our own way, instead. We look for so many things to fill the emptiness and to find the love we are longing for.

So did Adam and Eve's descendants. Once sin came into the world, people no longer had the intimate relationship with God that He desired and that they really longed for. So they, too, began to look to other things to fill the void.

And religion arrived on the scene.

Take a few minutes to think about the difference between having a religious affiliation and having a relationship with God. Name some characteristics that you think would identify each.

Religion	Relationship

1.2—THE LAW: THE CHARACTERISTICS OF SIN

I wasn't raised in a Christian home or in church. I always say we went to the First Church of Motown, because we spent our Sundays listening to music, cooking a big dinner (that's lunch for most of you), and going for an afternoon drive. Growing up, God was the furthest thing from my mind.

By the time I filled out that college application, my parents had divorced and my dad had moved away. I was pretty much living life on my own terms, but I sensed that there was something more. I had been to a few VBS's, had some experience with church on holidays, but I still didn't really know anything about God.

Remember the verse from yesterday, John 1:10? Jesus came into the world He created, but the world did not recognize Him. Let's look at John 1:11 today. It reads:

"He came to that which was His own, but His own did not receive Him."

Who were "His own"?

Why do you think that His own people, the Jews, did not receive Him?

Let's go back and find out what happened after Adam and Eve were driven from the Garden of Eden. You may remember that their son Cain killed their son Abel. Mankind became more and more wicked until God sent the flood to destroy all but Noah's family, because he was found to be righteous. Then God called Abraham, another righteous man, to be the father of a great nation, Israel.

Because of a famine they all ended up in Egypt until God led them out through Moses.

Let's begin by reading Exodus chapter 19 and 20:1-21. Why could the Israelites not look at God?

This is the same God who walked in the Garden with Adam and Eve prior to the Fall. He is a holy God building a relationship with an unholy people.

What does God give to Moses in chapter 20?

Why do you think the people needed these commandments?

The first four commandments are instructions about our relationship with God. The last six deal with our relationships with others.

Do you think God intended for these Laws to save them?

We cannot be in relationship with God until we first acknowledge our sin.

The Law was given as a moral compass for the Israelites and to show them their sin. Just as laws about driving show us what is right and wrong in order to keep us safe, these Laws were intended to open their eyes to what God expected of His people to keep them safe. Remember, these are the people He created and loved. He wanted a relationship with them, but He knew they were sinful creatures. The Law couldn't fix the problem; it only exposed it. Because

that is the first step for each of us. We cannot be in relationship with God until we first acknowledge our sin.

Let's go back and look at the Ten Commandments again in Exodus 20.

1. We are to have no other gods in our lives. The Israelites began to turn to the false gods of the people around them, because, remember, we all desire to worship something. God made us that way. Let's each look into our own hearts and see if we have put other "gods" ahead of the one true God. He should be our highest priority in life.

2. We are not to make idols of anything. The Israelites not only began to worship false gods, but they would actually make wooden or metal objects to worship that represented their gods. What things in our lives do we place above God? Do we have some objects, like tv's, cell phones, computers, music, books, etc., that we just cannot live without? Do we have some relationships that rank higher than God in our lives?

3. We are not to misuse the Lord's name. His name is holy. We misuse His name when we curse or say His name lightly or jokingly, or when we swear falsely by His name. Do we take the name of God lightly, either in our speech or in things we watch or listen to?

4. We are to remember the Sabbath day and keep it holy. The Jews' Sabbath was on Saturday, but most Christians celebrate the Sabbath on Sunday because the resurrection was on the first day of the week. Do we attend church to worship and set aside this day as holy while resting from our work?

5. We are to honor our mother and father. We are called to honor and respect our parents, even when we disagree with them. We are to treat them with dignity. Do we disrespect, disobey, or even speak negatively about our parents?

6. We are not to murder. Taking another person's life is a sin, but so is hating and being angry and unforgiving toward others, according to Jesus in Matthew chapter five. Do we have hatred, bitterness, or unforgiveness in our hearts toward another?

7. We are not to commit adultery. Adultery is taking another person's spouse as your own. Sex is a gift from God to be enjoyed between one man and one woman for life. According to Jesus in Matthew five, if we even look lustfully on someone

else, we have committed adultery in our hearts. Have we entertained lustful thoughts about someone other than our own spouse?

8. We are not to steal. We should never take something that belongs to someone else without permission, including someone else's ideas, work, creativity, etc. If we have copied cd's or movies without paying for them, it is stealing. If we have used someone else's ideas in a paper (plagiarism), it is stealing. Can we search our hearts for anything we've taken that was not our own?

9. We are not to give false testimony. We should not lie. Any time we say something that is not true, we are giving a false testimony. Have we told some untruths, even what we might consider "little white lies"?

10. We are not to covet anything that belongs to someone else. If we have a desire for something that is not ours, we are sinning. Why? Because we are basically admitting in our hearts that we are not satisfied with what God has given us. Notice that this is an inward desire of the heart, so even the condition of our hearts and our minds can be sin just as much as our outward deeds. Have we desired that which belongs to someone else?

So why are we looking at all of these Laws if they can't save us or give us a relationship with God? Because they reveal what is in us. They show us our inability to keep the Law and our need for a Savior. God is holy, and He desires for us to live a righteous life so that we can know Him. But the truth is that we are all sinners. Romans 3:23 says, "for all have sinned and fall short of the glory of God." We cannot enter into a personal relationship with the Lord Jesus Christ until we acknowledge and confess these sins before God.

The good news is that He is faithful to forgive us and cleanse us from all sin (1 John 1:9). So I ask you now to look into your heart and ask the Holy Spirit to expose anything that is sin in God's eyes. Then humbly ask Him to forgive you and cleanse you and help you to turn away from such sin. If you have never asked Jesus into your heart, now would be a good time! Ask God to save you and make you His child.

That is the first step to knowing Him. Unfortunately for the Israelites, the Law became a stumbling block to them. Remember how Jesus came and they didn't receive Him? By the time of Christ, the religious leaders had added many laws and taught that obeying those laws was what made them righteous.

They traded a relationship with God for a religious experience.

> How would that have affected their ability to recognize Jesus as the Messiah?

Think about your experience. Which of the following matches the closest to your Christian experience?

a. no experience with Christianity at all

b. some church attendance off and on

c. church member, but not active

d. religious church activity, but no personal relationship with God

e. daily personal relationship with God

Which do you feel is what God intends for you to have? Write a prayer to God below, asking Him to reveal to you what He wants you to understand about Himself.

1.3—THE TABERNACLE: THE COST OF SIN

Somewhere in my teenage years, I can recall having what I call a "God consciousness." I still didn't really know much about God, but I began to fear Him. I had a realization that certain things were wrong: drinking, cussing, and sex outside of marriage. I didn't refrain from all of those things, but I did become aware that those things were wrong, and I began to feel guilt when I sinned.

Part of that awareness, though, came with a dread that God didn't want me to have fun. Without knowing the Lord, I began to develop a "rules" mentality about Christianity.

Let's begin today by reading John 1:29. John the Baptist proclaimed Jesus as the Lamb of God who takes away the sins of the world.

Do you know where the imagery of a lamb is found in the Bible?

Yesterday we learned that God gave His Law so His people would understand His righteous requirements and so that they would be aware of their sin. God wanted His people to love, worship, and obey Him. His desire was for *relationship*. But His people could not keep the commandments because of their sinful nature. According to God's own righteous requirement, only the blood of a spotless animal could cover the sins of the people.

Read Hebrews 9:22. What does it say is required for sin to be forgiven?

Because the shedding of blood was necessary for the forgiveness of sins, God initiated sacrificial animal worship for the Israelites. This would often include a lamb without blemish or defect.

What did that look like? Today we will go back to Exodus and look at the tabernacle worship that God designed for His people as they wandered in the wilderness and as they settled in the Promised Land.

Let's begin with Exodus 25:1-9. Here we see God gave Moses specific instructions for the tabernacle, which would be a sanctuary in which His presence would dwell. In verse 8 God said that He would dwell among them. Again we see that God desired to have fellowship and dwell with His people.

Read Exodus 25:10-22. What did He command them to make?

He gave them instructions for building the tabernacle starting with the inside and moving out. The Ark of the Covenant or Testimony was to house the tablets containing the Ten Commandments. This would be located inside the tabernacle in the Most Holy Place. The Ark represented the covenant with them—that if they would obey His Law, He would be their God. Because God knew they would not be able to keep the Law completely because of their sinful nature, He made a way for the atonement of His people. The word "atonement" means that they are made "at one" with God again. The atonement cover on top of the Ark marked the place where God's presence literally would dwell (v.22).

Read Exodus 25:23-30. What were they commanded to make?

The table of the Bread of the Presence represented the presence of the One to come. Read John 6:25-40. Who is the Bread of Life?

Read Exodus 25:31-40. What were they instructed to make?

Read John 1:4-5, 9, 8:12, and 9:5. What does Jesus claim to be?

There are many, many more details about the tabernacle worship that pointed to Jesus, but for this study, we will not go into them all. Let's read one last thing about the tabernacle.

Read Exodus 29:42-46. What was the purpose of the bronze altar where the sacrifices were made at the entrance to the tabernacle?

This blood sacrifice was made as an offering of atonement, because only the blood could atone for the sins of the people. This blood would be applied to the altar as a sacrifice for the sins of the people, but it had to be done over and over, because it could never forgive them forever. This was a temporary system designed to do two things: cleanse the people of their sin so they could meet with their holy God and point the way to the Savior who, by His blood, would be able to save us once for all.

Remember that the point of the tabernacle was so that God could dwell in all of His glory among a sinful people. He desired to know them and for them to know Him.

Read John 1:14. The Greek for "made his dwelling" is closely related to the word for tabernacle. We could read this verse, "The Word became flesh and *tabernacled* among us." Jesus is the fulfillment of the tabernacle worship that the Jews had practiced for hundreds of years before His coming. It was meant to open their eyes to His presence among them. But for most of them, it didn't.

You see, just as today, the practice of religion seemed so holy and reverent, that men substituted the worship for the One we worship. They became so caught up in their "doing" for God that they didn't recognize His glory.

The tabernacle was all about worship in the presence of almighty God. It is most definitely a holy, reverent practice that only a priest could take part in. But everything about the tabernacle pointed to Jesus. God wanted His people to recognize His Son when He came to be the ultimate fulfillment of the sacrificial offering.

Remember John the Baptist's words in John 1:29? He recognized Jesus as the spotless Lamb of God, whose blood would be spilled to atone for the sins of the world.

Don't trade the thrill of truly knowing Jesus for the tragedy of just following religious practices. There is so much more.

My prayer for you today is that you would consider your relationship with God. If you have confessed your sins and asked Jesus into your heart, then understand that His desire is to know you and for you to know Him. Don't trade the thrill of truly knowing Jesus for the tragedy of just following religious practices. There is so much more.

Take a few minutes now to write a prayer to God, asking Him to reveal the truth of how you can know Him more.

1.4—THE PROPHETS: THE CONSEQUENCES OF SIN

Off to college I went, where I had less oversight and fear of being caught doing something wrong. I began to experiment with some of those things I thought would make me feel more grown-up or allow me to fit in better. The more independent I became, the less I feared God. I was blind to the truth of the consequences of sin. I began to ignore that God-awareness in me.

Let's read John 1:6-9, 19-28. According to 1:7-8, why did John the Baptist come?

In verses 19-23, the Pharisees were questioning John the Baptist about who he was. They wanted to know if he was Elijah, because Elijah never died but was taken to heaven by God. Many Jews believed that he would come back to announce the end of the world. Then they asked if he was the Prophet announced in Deuteronomy 18:15-18. This was likely referring to a series of Prophets after Moses who would speak for God to the people. He denied that he was Elijah or the Prophet.

Read Matthew 11:11-15 and 17:10-13. According to Jesus, John the Baptist *was* the fulfillment of the prophecy of Deuteronomy, despite his protests to the Pharisees. John the Baptist was attempting to deflect the attention from himself to Jesus. However, up until the time of John the Baptist, God sent many prophets to speak His word, warn of coming judgment, and prophesy of the coming Messiah. John the Baptist was that Prophet.

Read Isaiah 40:3. Now read again John 1:23. John the Baptist was the fulfillment of Isaiah's prophecy of one that would come to point the way to Jesus. Let's see what else the prophet Isaiah wrote.

Read Isaiah 53:1-12. Whom does this passage describe?

Turn to Isaiah 61:1-3. Now read Luke 4:16-21. Jesus basically tells them that He is the fulfillment of this prophecy. There are many, many more Messianic prophecies in the Old Testament (prophecies that specifically refer to the coming of Jesus). Here are just a few:

Birth of Christ: Micah 5:2; fulfillment in Matthew 2:1-6

Born of a virgin: Isaiah 7:14; fulfillment in Luke 1:35

Triumphal entry: Zechariah 9:9; fulfillment in Matthew 21:6-9

Betrayed by His follower: Psalm 41:9; fulfillment in John 13:18

Mocked and insulted: Psalm 22:7-8; fulfillment in Matthew 27:43

Death on a cross: Psalm 22:14-17; fulfillment in John 19:34

Lots cast for garments: Psalm 22:18; fulfillment in John 19:23

Bones would not be broken: Exodus 12:46; fulfillment in John 19:31-36

Raised from the dead: Psalm 16:10; fulfillment in John 20:9

Now, you may be asking yourself: "If the Jews had all of these prophecies regarding the coming of Christ, why did they not recognize Him as the Lord?" (Remember John 1:10-11).

First, let's answer this question: Why do you think God sent these prophets in the first place?

God sent the Law to show the Israelites their sin and His righteous requirements. God instituted the tabernacle worship to temporarily atone for their sin and to point to the One who would atone for sin once for all. God sent the Prophets to warn His people of the results of sin and to prepare their hearts for the coming Messiah. In all of this, He desires one thing: relationship with His people—to know and to be known. Once sin entered the human race, perfect relationship with God was forever marred; but because of His great love, He made a way to bring us back to Him.

So why did many of them not recognize or accept Him? For the same reason that many don't know Jesus today—religion gets in the way. Read John chapter nine. According to the *NIV Study Bible,* the Pharisees were "a legalistic and separatistic group who strictly, but often hypocritically, kept the law of Moses and the unwritten 'tradition of the elders.'"[ii] Remember how we said the Law became religion to them and they added hundreds more laws to what God gave to Moses? The Pharisees were a very religious group. They were the religious leaders of their day, well-educated, well-respected, and very important.

According to Jesus in John 9:39, they were spiritually blind. Jesus said His coming would make those who were blind (to sin) be able to see (their sin and repent); but those who claimed to see (the Pharisees) would become blind (to His truth).

Let's read John 12:37-43. The unbelief of the Pharisees fulfilled the prophecies of Isaiah. It wasn't that God kept them from believing and that they had no choice. They had a choice, but because they worshiped their own religious activities and traditions, and they loved the praise of men, they were blinded from seeing the truth: that Jesus really came to set them free. How sad that God did everything He could to draw His people to Himself, and yet they rejected the truth of knowing Him!

We will conclude on a sad note today, but one that is worth our pondering. Read Matthew chapter 23. Do the words of Christ pierce your heart? Can you hear the pain and passion in His voice? Why? Because these are His people that He loves! And they have rejected the One sent to save them.

Religion. It is spiritually blinding to those who submit to it—for those who seek church and rules and traditions, rather than just seeking God.

But there were those who truly believed in Jesus and followed Him. They knew Him as a Person. They listened to Him. They worshiped Him. They left everything to follow Him. So I ask you, do you know *about* God or do you truly *know* Him?

One last passage: Matthew 7:21-23.

Does He know *you*?

Do you know about God or do you truly know Him?

1.5—THE SON: THE CURE FOR SIN

One day, I visited a church with a guy I was dating at the time. I remember watching a girl sing as part of the service. Her eyes were closed and she had the most peaceful look on her face that I could ever recall seeing. I knew that deep inside, I didn't have that kind of peace. My heart longed to be at rest. I wanted what she had, and she sang about One named Jesus.

Again, let's look at the Gospel of John.

Read John 1:16-18. Copy verse 18 here:

This passage tells us that Jesus came to make the Father <u>known</u> to us.

So let's review what we have learned so far. God created Adam and Eve with free will and a desire to know Him. That fellowship was broken when they sinned. God sent the Ten Commandments so His people would recognize their sin and turn from it. God instituted sacrificial worship to show that "without the shedding of blood there is no forgiveness" (Hebrews 9:22b). And God sent the Prophets to speak for Him and turn His people back to Him. In all of these things, God is seeking fellowship with mankind.

Listen to the words of the prophet Jeremiah in 29:13. "You will seek me and find me when you seek me with all your heart." Hear the cry of God through the prophet. He just wants His people to seek Him with all their hearts. All of the acts of God in the Old Testament were to open their eyes to their need for a Savior whose blood could atone for sin and bring us all back into fellowship with God.

Let's read Romans 3:19-25a. How do we receive a righteousness apart from the Law?

Verse 24 says that we are "justified" freely by His grace. The word "justified" means "just-as-if-I'd" never sinned. Only the blood of God's Son could pay the price for our sin and bring us back into fellowship with God, just as if we had never sinned.

The Pharisees tried to achieve this righteousness or justification by observing the Law and being religious. They believed that if they kept all the Law and traditions of the elders (which none of them could do, but they liked to pretend that they did), then they were made right with God.

Read Matthew 5:17. Why did Jesus say He came?

Jesus was not saying that the Law was unimportant, but that it was supposed to reflect the inward motivations of the heart and not just an outward observance that was hypocritical and legalistic. God looks at the heart. But many of them had gotten so far from God, they didn't understand.

To many Israelites in Jesus' day, their traditions were more important than God's will. They didn't know Him personally. Remember, God's presence resided in the temple, which was a permanent structure that replaced the tabernacle. The glory of God was between the cherubim above the atonement seat of the ark of the testimony. This ark was located in the innermost room of the tabernacle called the Holy of Holies. Only the high priest could enter this room and only once a year on the Day of Atonement when he would take the blood of the sacrifice and place it on the mercy seat to atone for the sins of the people. So God must have seemed really far away to the people—unapproachable.

Read Matthew 27:50-51. This curtain was the one that separated the people from the Holy of Holies, and the tearing from top to bottom signifies that Christ's death on the cross made it possible for us to come into His presence.

Read Hebrews 4:14-16. How are we to come to God's throne?

Jesus Christ is the ultimate sacrifice for all sins, for all time. He is the Bridge that gives us access to the Father. Sin separates us from our holy, perfect God, but the blood of Jesus has made us right with God and given us a way to know Him.

We *can* know Him. We can *know* Him.

My prayer is that if you have made "church" your religion, you will take some time to consider Christ's work for you on the cross. All that He suffered and did for you was so that you could know Him intimately. Not as some far-off dictator in heaven who just condemns you because you can't keep His rules. He knows you can't keep His rules. That's why He sent His Son.

He knows you can't keep His rules. That's why He sent His Son.

WEEKEND DEVO: GOD'S DESIRE FOR RELATIONSHIP

Welcome to Weekend Devo! This is your time to rest in God's presence. No studying today—just meditating on the truths from Week One. So grab your cup of joe and let's get started.

This past week's lessons have all been about God's desire for relationship with every single person He ever created. That's amazing, isn't it? To think that the Creator of the Universe knows every one of us and wants us to know Him is really kind of mind-blowing. I know.

Years ago, I saw this "Top Ten" list on the internet: "Signs You're Falling in Love."

#10—You are comfortable and secure in your relationship and trust that your partner won't hurt you.

#9—You have remained together through good times and bad.

#8—You can be yourself with your partner more than any other person.

#7—You've forgotten your past relationships.

#6—You can't stop thinking about your partner and anticipate time together.

#5—You have great chemistry.

#4—You don't notice others as much.

#3—You love spending time together.

#2—Other priorities take a back seat.

#1—You start thinking about your future together.

We've all heard the phrase, "She worships the ground he walks on" used to describe someone madly in love. The truth is, we all desire to worship something or someone, and we all desire to be loved and pursued by someone greater than ourselves. Do you know why? Because we are made in the image of a God who desires to love and be loved.

The problem in our culture today is that we've done the same thing the Pharisees did: we've traded a Spirit-filled, loving relationship for cold, formal religion. And we're mostly okay with that because, honestly, it lets us get a foot in the door of the church, while still holding onto the world. Satan blinds us to truth, so we are deceived into thinking that's all there is or at least that's all we need.

Friend, we were created for spiritual intimacy. We don't like to think of that because God is supposed to be feared, and we shouldn't take Him so lightly or irreverently. Right? Yes, God is to be feared, but not in a distant, religious way. His Word is truth and we should fear Him and walk in His ways, but not because He'll kill us if we don't, but because we would be nothing without Him.

If you came to Christ because someone scared the hell out of you, let me share a few things with you today.

First, we are called the Bride of Christ. Just think about that for a minute. Marriage is extremely intimate.

"For your Maker is your husband—the Lord Almighty is his name—the Holy One of Israel is your Redeemer" (Isaiah 54:5).

"As a bridegroom rejoices over his bride, so will your God rejoice over you" (Isaiah 62:5b).

"Let us rejoice and be glad and give him glory! For the wedding of the Lamb has come, and his bride has made herself ready" (Revelation 19:7).

The Bible uses this marriage imagery for a reason: the Lord wants us to understand the intimate relationship that He desires to have with us.

Second, Jesus was not afraid of intimacy. In John 12 we read the story of a woman who took an expensive perfume and poured it on Jesus' feet and then wiped them with her hair. She did this to express her deep love and devotion to Him. This was an intimate act of worship that Jesus approved.

Third, the Apostle Paul in his letter to the Ephesians addresses the relationship between husbands and wives. Then he makes this statement: "This is a profound mystery—but I am talking about Christ and the church" (5:32). You see, we may not even understand this mystery, but the relationship between a husband and wife is meant to reflect the relationship between the Lord and us.

That is God's desire for the church! He wants us to know Him and love Him, not just go to church and try to "be good." I want to encourage you today that Jesus truly desires you. He has pursued you. He is in love with you and He wants you to know Him more. He is every girl's dream of a Warrior who fights for her, even unto death.

Let's look at that Top Ten List again. Can you answer these questions honestly in your heart today?

#10—Are you secure in your relationship with Jesus and trust that He will not hurt you?

#9—Have you stayed with Him through good times and bad?

#8—Do you feel that you can be yourself with Him?

#7—Have you let go of your past?

#6—Do you look forward to your daily time alone with Him?

#5—Do you have a deep love and passion for the Lord?

#4—Do you worry less about what others think?

#3—Do you love spending time with the Lord?

#2—Do other priorities take a back seat to your commitment to Him?

#1—Do you think about eternity with Him forever?

Are you in love with Jesus?

Because, beloved, He most assuredly is in love with you.

WEEK 2

God's Plan for Relationship

“NO ONE HAS EVER SEEN GOD, BUT GOD THE ONE AND ONLY, WHO IS AT THE FATHER’S SIDE, HAS MADE HIM KNOWN.”

JOHN 1:18-19

2.1—IT'S IN JESUS

I can't begin to tell you the difference in my life when I realized that all I longed for—forgiveness, acceptance, love, security, peace—could be found in Jesus! I began to spend time in His Word and worship Him until late into the night in my bedroom alone. I went to church, but my relationship with the Lord grew in my time alone with Him.

Let's look at some things that Jesus said while He was here on earth. We will read some selected passages in the Gospel of John. I want you to read them and then jot down a few words about what you think each passage means.

John 4:22

John 8:19

John 10:1-18

John 14:15-17

John 17:3

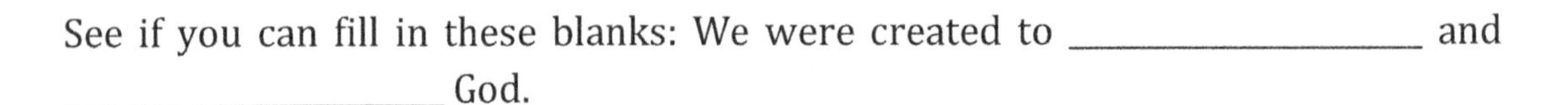

See if you can fill in these blanks: We were created to __________________ and __________________ God.

Did you get something like this? We were created to <u>know</u> and <u>love</u> God.

Let's read Psalm 139. Just let that sink in for a few minutes.

God knows us and He wants us to know Him. It has been said that we were created with a God-shaped vacuum that only He can fill. But many of us spend the majority of our lives trying to fill that vacuum with anything but God.

Why do you think that is? I want you to spend the next few minutes thinking about this. Why do we try to find fulfillment in anything but God? What are some of the things you have sought to fulfill you?

> If you're brave enough, could you list some of them here, just between you and God?

We all have done it. We all have sought ways to be satisfied in life apart from God. I think it's because finding fulfillment in God means that we give up the right to rule ourselves. And that goes against our human (but fallen) nature. We all desire to be the masters of our own fate. The problem with that philosophy is that we can't control our own fate. Only God is sovereign. He alone knows all things, controls all things, and can get us through all things.

He alone knows all things, controls all things, and can get us through all things.

God is the Creator of all, including you and me. He created us for a personal, intimate relationship with Himself. He put the need, desire, and longing within us to know Him. But because of our fallen nature, we rebel against His love and seek to find fulfillment in other things so that we can maintain the right to rule ourselves.

Over the next few days, we will look at a few of those substitutes for a relationship with God. Let's end our lesson today by writing a prayer to the Lord, asking Him to show us anything in our lives that we have substituted for a personal relationship with Him. Use Psalm 139 to guide your prayer.

2.2—IT'S NOT IN STUFF

According to the Scriptures, each of us was created to know and worship God, the Creator. He made us; He formed us exactly as we are, with all of our personality, talents, likes, and dislikes. According to Psalm 139, He knows us better than we know ourselves. He made us with a longing inside to know and love and serve Him, but somewhere along the way, many of us have turned elsewhere to have those longings met.

Yes, we are searching for something in life—peace, satisfaction, contentment, fulfillment—yet many of us don't realize that our search is for God. So as we grow up, we begin to look for things that will satisfy. It usually begins with material things, so that is where we will begin.

Name some material things that bring you happiness and pleasure:

Now, let me ask you this. What would you do if you woke up tomorrow and all of those things were gone?

Another question: After you have enjoyed those things for a while, does the longing go away, or do you still feel empty? Here's how you will know the answer to that question: Do you still need more?

Let's take a look at someone in the Bible who had to answer that question.

Read Matthew 19:16-29. At first glance, this story seems to be a little unfair. Just because the guy was rich, he couldn't get to heaven? But we must remember that Jesus saw his heart. So let's look at a few points here.

First, the man came up to Jesus and asked what "good thing" he must do to get eternal life. The fact that he came to Jesus tells us that he was probably searching for fulfillment in his life and looking for answers. He probably heard about this man Jesus and was taking a chance that He might *have* the answers. Also, he asked what "good thing" he must do.

What does this tell you about the young man's idea of salvation?

Now, Jesus' reply may surprise you, because it seems that Jesus was telling him that he could earn salvation by keeping the commandments. Again, we must remember that Jesus knew his heart. He was getting the young man to look at what was *in* his heart.

The young man then asked, "Which ones?" Did that make you smile a little? Apparently this young man was hoping he could just keep certain commandments to be okay. Notice that Jesus does give him a partial list of commandments.

Write them here:

The first five are from the Ten Commandments. Where does the sixth one come from? (Hint: Matthew 22:37-40)

Write below the commandments (from the Ten Commandments and from the two greatest commandments according to Jesus) that Jesus did **not** question him about:

So, Jesus left out the commandments about loving and worshiping God and about coveting. Why do you think that is?

This young man was Jewish and he knew the Law. I believe Jesus was making a point here about what this young man had sought to fill the emptiness inside: material things. Jesus wasn't telling him that his salvation was based on doing good works. Jesus was pointing out that his salvation was based on knowing and loving God, but the young man loved material things more. That's why Jesus told him to go and sell his possessions and give them to the poor. Jesus knew that this young man was not willing to give up his possessions to follow Him. It wasn't his wealth that kept him from eternal life. It was love for his wealth that kept him from loving and following Jesus.

Now read Matthew 19:22. What does this tell you about seeking material things to fill the emptiness in our souls?

The young man walked away sad. Still unfulfilled. Still lost. Still clutching to the things that he thought would bring him peace and contentment, and yet sad because he knew they hadn't. And they never will.

Months after I wrote this lesson, a friend of mine shared something interesting that she found about this passage. When the young man asks about what "good" thing he must do, the Aramaic translation (which many believe the *Gospel of Matthew* was originally written in and which is the language that Jesus actually spoke) used the word *tava*, from the Hebrew root, *tov. Tov* means "to be in harmony with God." So basically, Jesus answered the question of how to be in harmony with God.

"Come, follow me" (Matthew 19:21b).

The word *follow* in the Aramaic is *batar*, which means "cut into pieces or separate yourself" and "to be surrounded by."[iii] So, to have harmony (be in tune) with God, we must separate ourselves from those things that keep us from being surrounded by God. For the rich young ruler, it was his stuff, his worldly possessions. What is it for you and me?

We spend so much time, energy, and money on things, hoping that the next thing will be the one that satisfies. If I could just have________________________.

My friend, the truth is that there is no material thing on the face of this planet that will fulfill you, except the Word of God. That's the only tangible thing that I can think of. You know why that is? Because John 1:14 tells us that Jesus is the Word made flesh. When we interact with the Word of God, we are interacting with Jesus Himself, and that, my friend, will fulfill.

There is no material thing on the face of this planet that will fulfill you except the Word of God.

2.3—IT'S NOT IN PEOPLE

There are many things that we seek to fill the emptiness inside. Because I felt rejected by my father, I turned to a boyfriend to give me the acceptance I craved. But even that relationship couldn't fill my longings. This brings to mind another woman who went through many relationships, looking for fulfillment and peace.

Read John 4:1-18. According to Jewish tradition, a woman could be divorced only in the case of marital unfaithfulness, and only two or three times at the most. She could have had a husband who died, after which she remarried, but the fact that she was now living with a man she was *not* married to, tells us that she had some immorality in her life.

Why do you think this woman had five husbands and was now living with man number six?

Why do you think Jesus told her to go call her husband and come back?

Just as he did with the rich young ruler, Jesus was helping her to see for herself the bad choices that she had made, but he was not condemning her.

What did Jesus offer her (verse 10)?

Why do you think Jesus offered her this?

This woman had a longing that she had tried many times to fill with relationships with men. But these relationships never could satisfy her real need. Jesus described this need as a thirst—an intense longing and desire for something to quench the emptiness in her soul.

What do you think He meant by His statement to her in verse 13?

He was making it clear to her that her thirst would never be satisfied with a continual stream of men in her life. Only Jesus, the Living Water, could satisfy her deepest need so that she would never thirst again.

Read each of the following Scriptures and jot down what you think they mean:

Psalm 42:1

Isaiah 55:1

John 7:38

Revelation 7:17

Revelation 21:6

Our culture today tells us that all we need is to find that perfect someone who will meet all our needs. We will be completely satisfied and fulfilled once we find our soul mate. The truth is that there is no one on the planet who can meet our deepest need. We will end up like the woman at the well, lonely and unsatisfied, still looking for just the right one.

We each have a deep longing, a need to be fulfilled, that can only be satisfied in Jesus. He is the Living Water that quenches our thirst. When we learn how to depend on Him and spend time with Him and trust our lives to Him, we will find a place of peace and joy and satisfaction that no one can take away and no one else can replace.

Don't look for someone else to fill what only God can fill in your life. You will be left lonely and sad, still searching like the woman at the well. But let's look at the rest of her story.

Don't look for someone else to fill what only God can fill in your life.

Read John 4:27-42. Notice that she left her water jar behind when she went to tell everyone about Jesus. She may have asked others if He could be the Christ, but deep down, she already knew. Because she no longer needed the water that leaves us thirsty. She had the Living Water, and she knew that she would never thirst again.

What about you? Are you still looking for others to fulfill you? You may be wondering how you can find fulfillment in Someone that you can't see or touch as opposed to a real, live person who can hold and comfort you. It comes through spending time with the living God. We may not see Him, but we can know and interact with Him through His Word. When you really begin to seek God, you will hear His voice and feel His presence. He will bring you a level of comfort that you could never get from someone's arms. This relationship with Jesus comes first by submitting your life completely to Him and trusting Him to save you. Then you seek Him by reading His Word and praying. Listen to Christian music. Get quiet and ask Him to speak to you. You will begin to experience Him in your life in a way that is more real than the person sitting in front of you.

"Taste and see that the Lord is good; blessed is the man who takes refuge in him" (Psalm 34:8).

That is my prayer for you, my friend. If you have merely tasted church and religious activity, but you have never experienced this Living Water in Jesus, then like the woman at the well, I invite you to come see this Man.

2.4—IT'S NOT IN ME

So far we have learned that we all long to be fulfilled and satisfied in life. God created us that way. But the enemy works hard to convince us that we can have those needs filled in ways other than in God. Many of us seek to find fulfillment in achievements. If we can work hard enough, be smart enough, athletic enough, perfect enough . . . then maybe we can win the approval and acceptance of others that we crave.

Today we are going to look at the life of Paul the Apostle, who wrote most of the New Testament. Let's look at his life before he came to know Jesus.

> Read the following passages: Acts 22:3-5, Acts 26:4-11, Galatians 1:13-14, and Philippians 3:4-6. What can you conclude about Paul's life from these passages?

Of course, we don't know all there is to know about Paul (formerly Saul) prior to His coming to Christ, but I think we can safely say that he was doing all that he could to be approved and accepted within the Jewish faith, and specifically among the Pharisees. The Pharisees (whom we read about earlier) were a specific sect among the Jews who believed in strict adherence to the Law of Moses, but they also had added hundreds of laws to that. They loved outward appearances that made them appear important. They held to the letter of the Law but missed the spirit of the Law that God intended.

The Pharisees trusted in their own righteousness to save them. In essence, they filled their emptiness inside with achievements that would win them the approval, acceptance, and importance that they longed for. And they missed the whole truth of Jesus when He came.

How about you? Do you seek to fill your inner longing for acceptance and wholeness with achievements and awards? Do you feel that if you can do enough to make others proud of you or make friends accept you, then you will be fulfilled with their praise and honor of you? If so, then you need to have an encounter with Jesus like Paul did.

Read the rest of his story in Acts 22:6-16. Now read what Paul said in Philippians 3:4-11.

> How did Paul say all of his accomplishments as a Pharisee compared to his knowing Christ?

Take a few minutes and think about all that you have gained or accomplished as a student, wife, mother, worker, church member.

> Write below all that you have achieved and could put confidence in as Paul once did.

> If you lost all of those achievements, accolades, or the approval of others tomorrow, would you be devastated?

> If no one noticed or gave you credit for the great things you've done, would you be hurt?

Do you compare your "work" to others and always feel that you fall short?

Paul came to know Jesus in such a way that he considered all he had gained and achieved as trash compared to knowing Jesus. Paul came to the understanding that his desires could never be fulfilled no matter how hard he tried to be a good Pharisee. All of the importance and acceptance and having the approval of his parents and teachers—none of it meant anything because those things could never fill the emptiness inside. Only Jesus can do that.

Read the words of Paul in Ephesians 1:18-23. Look again at verse 23: "the fullness of him who fills everything in every way." Only Jesus fills us completely. You will never be satisfied in life apart from Him.

Only Jesus fills us completely.

2.5—IT'S NOT IN RELIGION

We have looked at several things that humans look to for fulfillment: material things, relationships, achievements, acceptance, and approval. Today I want us to look at one more area, because this is the one that I believe is the most dangerous.

Many people look to religion to satisfy. Again, when I use the term *religion*, I am referring to the connotative meaning in our culture today of "going to church." The danger is that because of religion's discipline and Satan's deception, religion will work for a little while.

Religion offers several things. First, if one is living a life that is out of control and full of sin, religion will bring some stability. People sometimes decide to get involved in church and stop a sinful lifestyle. It brings a sense of stability and discipline into their lives for a while, because they have a set of rules to follow. Any religion will do this.

Second, religion will give one a sense of hope and direction. By going to church, many people feel that they are doing something right. They may give money, serve in the church, and participate in activities that make them feel better about themselves and feel that their lives are more worthwhile. Any religion based on works will do this.

Third, religion will give one a new set of friends and acquaintances. Going to church or a place of worship will open doors of opportunity to be involved with like-minded people. It gives one a sense of belonging and acceptance. Again, even joining a gang can do this.

> *Satan uses the illusion of religion to satisfy people temporarily until he can convince them that's all there is!*

So what is the problem with religion? Isn't going to church good if it gives people hope, direction, friends, discipline, etc.? The problem is that false religion is a lie from the enemy. *Satan uses the illusion of religion to satisfy people temporarily until he can convince them that that is all there is!*

When we can no longer keep up the illusion of righteousness; when we can't keep up the good works; when the new friends turn on us; when the place of worship gets stale and boring; and when we realize our life really is no better than it was before, dissatisfaction with religion sets in. And people walk away.

I want to share seven reasons that I believe religion (as we have defined it in this study) doesn't work.

1. You can go to church and never know whom you worship.

> Read Acts 17:22-24. What did the Athenians have inscribed on their altar?

Paul told them they were very *religious.* The word used for religious here can also be translated *superstitious.* In other words, they used religion as a tool to keep from offending some unknown God. Haven't we done the same in our culture today? We go to church and get our name on the roll so we can have our get-out-of-hell ticket punched each week, but do we even know the God we claim to worship?

2. You can be aware of everybody's sin but your own.

> Read Luke 18:9-14. What did the Pharisee think about the tax collector? What do you think the Pharisee thought about himself?

Religion will quickly draw us into self-righteousness. Apart from God, we cannot obey Him. Religion will quickly lead us to look for faults in others to make us feel better about our own failure.

3. You can know the Word but not walk in it.

Read James 1:22-24. What did James use to describe the deception of hearing but not obeying the Word?

The other response to hearing God's Word apart from a relationship with Him is to ignore it. Many in our churches do this every week.

4. You can pray to God but never truly seek Him.

Read Matthew 6:5. Why did the hypocrites pray in the synagogues and on the street corners?

Religion will cause us to seek our own will rather than God's.

5. You can try to follow the rules but never follow Jesus.

Read Matthew 15:1-9. What did Jesus say in verse 6 the Pharisees did for the sake of their traditions?

Religion will lead us to value our own rules and traditions above God's. We will seek ways to continue to appear godly without actually being accountable to God.

6. You can look right but not be right.

Read 2 Timothy 3:1-5. Describe how someone can have a "form of godliness" but deny its power.

Religion will hide behind a mask of spirituality.

7. You can sacrifice your time and even money but never sacrifice your life.

Read 1 Samuel 15:22. What does God consider a true sacrifice?

God doesn't need our time or money. He only wants our hearts.

I hope by now you can agree that religion in and of itself is only a sham. You can be Buddhist, Muslim, Hindu, or go to a local Christian church and get the same result: stability, direction, discipline, belonging, and acceptance. It will work for a little while. That's part of Satan's strategy. But in the end, you'll be left in chaos, confusion, disillusion, and loneliness apart from a relationship with Jesus Christ. That's why we see so many people fall away from the church. They've tried religion. They haven't tried Jesus.

Only a relationship in which you surrender your life to the King of kings will give you what you are truly longing for—peace with God and eternal life. That's why we praise Him. He alone is worthy.

Take some time to consider your relationship with God and with church. Have you ever been dissatisfied with church and wanted to walk away? I don't mean change churches, but actually give up on God. Would you prayerfully consider if you have sought religion rather than the Savior?

WEEKEND DEVO:
GOD'S PLAN FOR RELATIONSHIP

Don't you love having a day to just sit at His feet and soak in His presence? I hope you are able to set aside a time each week that is longer than your normal quiet time and just rest in Him.

Augustine of Hippo was a Christian theologian who lived in the fourth and fifth centuries. In his book, *Confessions*, Augustine wrote, "You move us to delight in praising You; for You have formed us for Yourself, and our hearts are restless till they find rest in You."[iv]

Isn't that beautiful? The truth is that we may spend a lifetime searching in all the things of the world, seeking to find rest and fulfillment, but we will not be still until we surrender to the One who made us, loves us, died for us, and is interceding for us as the right hand of the Father.

From our studies this week, we saw that some responded to Jesus' call to intimacy with surrender, such as the woman at the well. But some walked away sad, and some rejected Him completely.

Beloved, we all have a choice in how we respond to Jesus.

I think many resist Him because we are afraid of losing our right to do our own thing. There was a time in my life that I felt that way, too, until I understood the Lord's desire for intimacy with me.

I can remember the moment that I discovered this truth. I was reading a book entitled *Sacred Obsession* by Becky Tirabassi in which she writes, "What you chase after, you become . . . whether it is holy or unholy."[v]

In our last Weekend Devo, we talked about intimacy with the Lord. I want to pick up on that theme today by looking at the Song of Solomon. The Song of Solomon was written by King Solomon over 3000 years ago and before his spiritual decline. The book is a poetic description of Solomon's betrothal to the Shulamite maiden. The natural interpretation of this book is that it describes the beauty of married love.

But for centuries, the Song was believed to be a spiritual description of the love of God for His people.[vi] Only in the last two hundred years has it been interpreted as only a description of married love. I believe it is both.

Luke 24:27 says that ALL the Scriptures are concerning Jesus. That tells me that even the Song of Solomon reveals Jesus to us; therefore, I believe this beautiful love story is a spiritual description of the intimacy of love between Jesus the Bridegroom and His beautiful bride—you and me.

You see, we are described in the Bible as being betrothed to Jesus.

"I am jealous for you with a godly jealousy. I promised you to one husband, to Christ, so that I might present you as a pure virgin to him" (2 Corinthians 11:2). A betrothal was akin to an engagement period, except that it was legally binding. When we are in a relationship with Jesus, we are promised to Him, betrothed to Him, engaged to Him. We are awakening to love and maturing in that love.

The consummation of this relationship takes place at the Second Coming, as we read in Revelation 19:7:

"Let us rejoice and be glad and give him the glory! For the wedding of the Lamb has come, and his bride has made herself ready."

You and I, friends, are the bride. Our time here on earth is like the dating period. We are drawn to the Lord by His love and kindness. We enter into an intimate, personal relationship with the Lord in which we are getting to know Him better and falling deeper and deeper in love with Him.

"I love the Lord, for he heard my voice; he heard my cry for mercy. Because he turned his ear to me, I will call on him as long as I live" (Psalm 116:1-2).

I want to encourage you today, that if you have answered the Lord's invitation to follow Him, then you have entered into the most intimate and personal relationship that you can ever have. Jesus is courting you; He is calling to you to come and spend time with Him every day. He wants you to know Him more. He wants to be with you and comfort you and love on you. Our relationship as the bride of Christ and the Bridegroom is the greatest romance ever!

In a culture that is obsessed with sex, Satan has perverted the wholesomeness of romance. Don't let that cause you to shy away from intimacy with Jesus. Sex within the context of marriage is simply a reflection of the oneness that God desires with us. Just as sexual love produces oneness with our spouse and the fruit of our womb, intimacy with Jesus produces oneness with Him and the fruit of the Spirit.

This place of intimacy with the Lord is about entering into the secret place, the Holy of Holies, in worship, prayer, and the Word. Did you know that in Jewish tradition, the three books of Solomon were believed to represent the temple that Solomon built? Proverbs represents the Outer Court; Ecclesiastes represents the Inner Court; and the Song of Solomon represents the Holy of Holies, the very place where the presence of God dwelled.[vii]

God wants you to come into the Holy of Holies with Him, the intimate place where He dwells. There He will meet with you and speak to you through His Word. He will touch your spirit and your soul in ways that you cannot imagine. I want to walk through the Song of Solomon with you, but for now, just know that God has written a love song for you.

Because He's in love with you.

"The Lord your God is with you, he is mighty to save. He will take great delight in you, he will quiet you with his love, he will rejoice over you with singing" (Zephaniah 3:17).

WEEK 3

God's Provision in Relationship

“HIS DIVINE POWER HAS GIVEN US EVERYTHING WE NEED FOR LIFE AND GODLINESS THROUGH OUR KNOWLEDGE OF HIM WHO CALLED US BY HIS OWN GLORY AND GRACE.”

1 PETER 1:3

3.1—HIS FORGIVENESS

By this point, I hope you are convinced that what you need is not religion, but a relationship with the Lord Jesus Christ. So what does that look like and how does it fulfill? I'm glad you asked!

If you have never surrendered your life to Jesus, then that is the first place to start. Let's look at a few verses in Romans.

Jot down what each one says in your own words.

Romans 3:10

Romans 3:23

These two verses sum up the very important truth that we are all sinners. No one can claim that he has not sinned.

1 John 1:8 says, "If we claim to be without sin, we deceive ourselves and the truth is not in us." That's good news because it puts us all in the same boat! You have the same problem everyone else in the world has: You are a sinner. Remember Adam and Eve in the Garden? Their rebellion brought sin into the world, and now we are all born with a sinful nature.

Read Romans 5:12 and write here what you think it means.

Remember that in the Garden, Adam and Eve were told that if they ate of the fruit from the tree of knowledge they would surely die. It wasn't that the fruit killed them like a poison. It was their sin that brought spiritual and physical death. God intended for them to live forever, but after their sin, physical death came to their bodies. So the consequence of sin is death.

Romans 6:23 says "For the wages of sin is death." It may sound harsh to us, but sin actually brings death into our lives—both spiritually and physically. A wage is something you earn. Our sin leads to consequences that bring separation between us and God—the only source of true love, joy, and peace (life). And our sin leads to our ultimate physical death so that we die on this earth and face only judgment and pain.

Turn to Hebrews 9:27 and jot down what it says.

Why do we die and then face judgment? Think about all you read in the first week of this study. God created us and did everything possible to provide salvation and relationship with Himself through His Son. If we reject His Son and die in our sin, then we have chosen death and judgment rather than the love of the God who created us.

But the good news is that we don't have to! Look at the rest of Romans 6:23.

"For the wages of sin is death, *but the gift of God is eternal life in Christ Jesus our Lord.*" Isn't that exciting?? A gift is something you don't earn but you are given because someone loves you and wants to bless you. That Someone is God! He knows the price of our sin, and He was willing to pay the price Himself so that you could know Him and be with Him forever!

Read Romans 5:8 and copy it here.

While we were still sinners! Not once we got everything right in our lives and decided to do the right thing. While we were *still* sinners, Christ died for us. Not because we earned it or deserved it (we didn't!). Only because of the great love that God has for us and His desire that we would have intimate fellowship with Him.

So how can you accept this gift from God? It's very simple.

Romans 10:9-13 says "that if you confess with your mouth, 'Jesus is Lord,' and believe in your heart that God raised him from the dead, you will be saved. For it is with your heart that you believe and are justified, and it is with your mouth that you confess and are saved. As the Scripture says, 'Anyone who trusts in him will never be put to shame.' For there is no difference between Jew and Gentile—the same Lord is Lord of all and richly blesses all who call on him, for 'everyone who calls on the name of the Lord will be saved.'"

So, if you believe that God the Father sent His Son Jesus to earth to live and teach and die on the cross to pay the penalty for your sins, and if you believe that God raised Him from the dead and that He is Lord, then you simply need to confess it out loud and you will be saved. You call on His name, accept His gift, and submit to His Lordship.

We first have to agree with God about our sins. Psalm 51 is a great place to start. This Psalm is the prayer of David when he confessed his sins to God. Turn there now and read through the Psalm.

In verse 6, where does David say that God desires truth?

Salvation comes as we allow God to show us the truth about ourselves, and we agree with Him that our sin is wrong. Make this Psalm your prayer to God. He truly wants to change us from the inside out.

If you have never truly believed in your heart, repented of your sins, and confessed Jesus as your Lord, then I invite you to do so right now. Not to join a church. Not to get religion. Not to turn your life around. Not to make a commitment to do better. Just to make Jesus your Lord and Savior. That's all. He will do the rest. Just pray this prayer from your heart:

Salvation comes as we allow God to show us the truth about ourselves, and we agree with Him that our sin is wrong.

"Lord Jesus, I believe that You truly are the Son of God and that You died for my sins and rose again. I believe that You are Lord of all, and I invite You to come into my heart. Save me from my sins and make me a new creature in You. I surrender my life completely to You as my Lord, and I will live for You."

If you prayed that prayer for the first time and truly meant it, then welcome to the family! You have entered into the most personal, life-giving, intimate relationship that you will ever know. If you have already given your life to Jesus, then I pray you will use today's lesson to evaluate your walk with the Lord. Ask Him to show you any area of your life that is not submitted to His Lordship.

"I waited patiently for the LORD; he turned to me and heard my cry. He lifted me out of the slimy pit, out of the mud and mire; he set my feet on a rock and gave me a firm place to stand. He put a new song in my mouth, a hymn of praise to our God" (Psalm 40:1-3a).

That's what God has done for you and me.

3.2—HIS INTIMACY

You know, after I prayed the prayer of faith and asked Jesus to be my Lord and Savior, my life didn't just change overnight. I know some people who experienced miraculous deliverance from sin at the moment of conversion, but my journey was a gradual one. The broken places needed time to heal, but God was patient with me.

Maybe you have been a Christian for a long time but never really enjoyed the kind of love and intimacy with the Lord that we have been talking about. Or maybe you have given your life completely to Jesus and trusted Him for your salvation for the first time. How do you experience the Living Water which satisfies so that you will never thirst again? Your circumstances haven't changed. You still have the same family, same friends, same problems you had before, so what is different? You are, my friend.

You may not feel any different at all. Or maybe you do feel completely free from the burden of sin. Either way, the first thing you will want to do is the same thing you would experience if you developed a relationship with a new friend: talk to Him! Whether you've never prayed before or have been praying all your life, God can take us all to new levels with Him.

Many people feel as if they don't know how to pray, but we know how to talk to a friend, right? It's the same thing, only you are now talking to the King of the universe! Sounds scary, but it shouldn't be. Remember when Jesus died on the cross and the temple curtain was torn, giving us access to the Holy of Holies? That means that even though God is to be feared because He is King of the universe, He has given us the right, as His children, to come boldly to His throne.

Read Hebrews 4:16 and jot down what it says to you.

This confidence we have is simply the belief that God loves us and wants to hear our prayers, and the assurance that we are truly saved and have eternal life.

How does 1 John 5:11 give us that assurance?

Do not allow the enemy (Satan) to cause you to doubt your salvation. If you truly believe in your heart and confessed it with your mouth, then you are saved.

According to 1 John 5:14, what does that assurance give us?

Notice it says, "according to his will." So how do we know what is according to His will? As you spend time with the Lord as you would a close friend, and as you read His Word, you will begin to discern what His will is. His will won't contradict His Word.

Read 1 Peter 5:7 and Philippians 4:6-7. What do these verses tell you about prayer?

When the disciples didn't know how to pray, they asked Jesus to teach them. Let's look at what He said.

Read Luke 11:1-4. The first thing Jesus taught them was to acknowledge that God is holy (v. 2). That is what *hallowed* means. Jesus was teaching His disciples that even though He is our Friend and we can approach Him with confidence any time, we still must come into His presence as if we are on holy ground. He is holy and mighty, King of kings and Lord of lords. He is our Savior, Redeemer, Healer, Deliverer, and Provider. He is gracious and compassionate, but He is also righteous and just. We humble ourselves before Him and surrender to His authority because we trust His heart for us.

I love to think of a prince or princess coming into the presence of the king. He is feared all over his kingdom because he rules over all, yet his children can come into his presence any time because he delights in them and wants to hear their requests. That's our relationship with the Father. He is to be feared and honored because He reigns over all the universe; yet as His children, we can come boldly to His throne of grace.

...yet as His children, we can come boldly to His throne of grace.

Next, Jesus told His disciples to pray for God's kingdom to come (v. 2). What does that mean? God's kingdom is everywhere that He rules. And while we know that God is sovereign, meaning that He rules and reigns over everything, we also know that Satan has a lot of influence in our world. We will talk more about the enemy later, but for now, praying for God's kingdom to come means we want God to rule and reign over everything in our world and in our lives. We are submitting our will to His will.

Then, Jesus taught His disciples to pray for their daily bread (v. 3). Whether He meant actual physical food or spiritual food, I think the point is that we only need enough for today. When God fed the Israelites in the wilderness, He gave them enough manna for one day. No matter what our needs are, we are to learn to depend on Him one day at a time.

Next, Jesus taught the disciples to ask God to forgive their sins (v. 4). Even after we are saved, we are still sinners in need of His grace. We should keep short accounts with God, meaning that as soon as we are aware that we have sinned, we should pray and ask for forgiveness. We should do our best to not sin intentionally, because we love God and want to please Him, but when we do sin, we should confess and turn away from that sin.

Then, Jesus taught His disciples to forgive those who had sinned against them (v. 4). Forgiveness is not always easy. It's hard to forgive when people hurt us, especially if they continue to hurt us and not ask for forgiveness. Nevertheless, that is what God expects us to do. Why? Because He has shown mercy and forgiveness to us.

Last, Jesus taught the disciples to pray that God would lead them not into temptation (v.4). This verse doesn't mean that God tempts us (James 1:13-14) but that we are asking God to lead us out of tempting situations (1 Corinthians 10:13).

Whether you are new to the faith or have been living for Jesus for years, God wants us to seek His face daily in quiet times of prayer, sharing our hearts with Him, and listening for His voice.

So enjoy your time getting to know God. Talk to Him throughout the day as you would to a close friend. Spend time listening as well. A conversation should never be one-sided. As you begin to share your love with Him, your burdens with Him, and your day with Him, Jesus will begin to speak to you and comfort you, and you will begin to experience that Living Water that will well up in you until it overflows.

One great habit you can make is to take time to journal what you believe the Lord is speaking to you through His Word and your quiet time listening to Him. If you have more questions about what it looks like to establish daily habits and patterns of seeking Him, you can check out my best-selling book, *Seek Him First: How to Hear from God, Walk in His Will, and Change Your World.*

Take some time now and write a prayer to God, asking Him to draw you closer to Him in prayer and intimacy.

3.3—HIS TRUTH

One of the greatest ways to get to know Jesus and enjoy your relationship with Him is to fall in love with His Word. I remember the hunger and thirst I had for God's Word when I first got saved. I couldn't wait to get to church and sit under my pastor's teaching. I highlighted Bible passages and took notes in a journal, and I still do that today.

Remember John 1:14? Jesus is the word made flesh, so when we read His Word, we are interacting with Jesus Himself.

The Bible is the revelation of God to us. It reveals to us who God is and the love He has for us. First, let's look at some verses about the word of God. Read each one and jot down a few words about each.

2 Samuel 22:31

Psalm 119:105

Isaiah 55:11

John 17:17

Ephesians 6:17

2 Timothy 3:16

Hebrews 4:12

These are just a few Scriptures, but I hope they whet your appetite for God's Word. These Scriptures tell us that God's Word is perfect. There are no mistakes or contradictions in it, from Genesis to Revelation. His Word will show us the way to go. God's Word is all true. It is a weapon for the believer. All of it was written by God. The Bible is alive and can penetrate our hearts and show us things about ourselves.

Even if you don't like to read, doesn't that sound intriguing? There's never been another book like the Bible. It has stood the test of time, been the best-selling book ever, and people have died to protect it. It isn't magic, but it is supernatural. God will reveal Himself to you and speak to you through His Word. That is another way that we connect with Him and grow in our relationship with Him.

God will reveal Himself to you and speak to you through His Word.

Today we have the pure, unadulterated word of God in tons of versions, with study notes and all kinds of helps, so that we can understand and apply it to our lives. And if you ask Jesus to help you understand and to speak to you through His Word, He will.

As I always say, if you don't understand something in the Bible, just do the things you do understand, and God will reveal the rest in time. He will take you on an exciting adventure of faith as you dig into His Word.

One of the most exciting things to me about the Word of God is the power it has in our lives when we believe it and speak it. I don't just read and study the Word; I memorize and confess it over my life, my family, and my circumstances. Jot down what each of these Scriptures is saying to you.

Psalm 119:11

Isaiah 55:11

Proverbs 3:1, 3

Colossians 3:16

These verses tell us that having God's Word in our hearts (memorization), going out from our mouths (confession), and dwelling within us as we worship and work for the Lord will accomplish great things for the Kingdom of God. God's Word is powerful. Pray before you read it. Study it, memorize it, and confess it over your life.

His Word is the truth that we all need for our lives. Come get to know God through His Word. You will never be the same.

3.4—HIS SPIRIT

So, today let's continue to discover what it means to have a relationship with Jesus. We have learned so far that we can come to Him at anytime, anywhere, and get to know Him. We can spend time with Him and talk with Him. We can read His Word and get to know Him. But what happens when we sin? We are not perfect, so obviously we are going to make mistakes.

God knows that we are not perfect, and He is able to handle all our sin and mistakes. When Jesus died on the cross, He died for all our sins—past, present, and future. So our sins are already covered by the blood of Jesus. When we sin, it separates us from God and keeps us from being in His presence and hearing His voice. Confession of those sins brings forgiveness and brings us back into fellowship with Him.

What we want to learn today is the role of the Holy Spirit in our relationship with God. Who is the Holy Spirit? He is the third person of the Trinity. The Bible teaches us that God is three-in-one. It's a difficult concept to understand—a holy mystery! But God exists as three persons: the Father, Son, and Holy Spirit.

We pray to the Father, we ask in Jesus' name, and we enlist the help of the Holy Spirit. The Holy Spirit is the very Spirit of God who comes to live inside us at the moment of salvation. He is the power within us to help us live for God. Let's look at a few Scriptures and jot down what you learn from each:

John 14:26

John 16:13

Acts 1:8

We see through these verses that the Holy Spirit, or Comforter, comes to live in believers, and He guides us into all truth. Let's look at another passage that talks about life in the Spirit.

Read Romans 8:1-17. What do these verses tell us about our role along with the Holy Spirit?

We aren't perfect when we become Christians, but this passage is clear that we do have the choice to live by the Spirit rather than being controlled by our sinful nature. It's not about rules and regulations—that's religion. Our good works don't earn us salvation—that's religion. Instead, it's about the God who loves us and made a way to save us, coming to live inside us, so we could have the power to walk with Him. Isn't that incredible?

I don't think religion can offer that kind of miracle. God made the way for us to know Him through His Son Jesus. He made the way for us to live for Him through His Holy Spirit. When we fail, He made the way to draw us back through both: the Holy Spirit will convict us of sin, and Jesus' blood will cover our sin. God is holy and we can only be in His presence when we are cleansed. Thank God He made the way for that to be possible!

Let's read a few more verses and jot down what they mean to you.

Romans 8:26-27

1 Corinthians 6:19-20

Ephesians 1:13-14

Ephesians 2:22

The very Spirit of God, present at Creation, living in Jesus when He walked this earth, lives inside of you if you belong to Jesus. That is a miracle that we shouldn't take lightly. God comes to dwell within us to lead, guide, comfort, convict, teach, help, direct, and empower. Hallelujah! What more could we ask?

Surrender to the Spirit of God and allow Him to lead you and guide you. Respond to His conviction. Follow His leadership. Cooperate with the Spirit's work within you.

The power of the Holy Spirit within us is a great gift from God. Why don't you write a prayer of thanks to the Lord today for making a way for Him to live within you?

God comes to dwell within us to lead, guide, comfort, convict, teach, help, direct, and empower.

3.5—HIS RIGHTEOUSNESS

Let's end our week with one more aspect of what a relationship with God looks like. So far we have learned that we come to Him and surrender our lives to His Lordship, pray to stay in communication with Him, read His Word to hear His voice and learn more about Him, and rely on the presence of the Holy Spirit within to guide and teach us. We need to look at one more aspect of this relationship: holiness.

What is holiness? We know that God is Holy and we are human, so how can we have this attribute of God? Holiness is about living a lifestyle that is pleasing to God. You may think, "That sounds more like religion!" But I am going to show you the difference.

We can strive in our own power to live a righteous life or we can surrender to the power of the Holy Spirit within us and, by faith, trust Him to live a righteous life through us.

Let's look at two words: justification and sanctification.

Remember we said that to be justified means "just-as-if-I'd" never sinned? Let's look at a few verses about that.

Remember Romans 3:23? Now read Romans 3:24 and write it here:

Read Romans 5:1-2 and Romans 10:10. What do these verses tell you?

In other words, we are justified, or made to be in right standing with God, not because we do right things, but completely by faith in God's grace as shown to us through Jesus.

Now let's look at sanctification. To be sanctified means to be set apart by the work of the Holy Spirit within us. Let's look at a few Scriptures.

Read 1 Corinthians 1:2 and note what that verse is saying.

We are called to be holy, set apart, sanctified in Christ Jesus. This calling is not about following a bunch of rules, but simply about following Jesus. The word *disciple* means a "fully devoted follower." That's what we are in Christ—sanctified and set apart as belonging to Him.

Every day we have opportunities to walk in the Spirit or in the flesh.

So what is our part in holiness? We are the ones who have a free will and the ability to choose whether or not we will follow Jesus. Every day we have opportunities to walk in the Spirit or the flesh. What does that mean?

Remember Romans 8:1-17 from yesterday? We see from this passage that Jesus sets us free from the law of sin and death, and then He gives us the freedom to walk, not according to the flesh, or our sinful nature, but according to the Spirit of God within us. This Spirit-filled life is not forced on us. We still get to choose.

Read Galatians 5:16-26. Here we see again that God is calling us to live by the Spirit and not the sinful nature. Why? Because we are in a relationship now with One who is holy. He loves us enough to die for us and to do everything in His

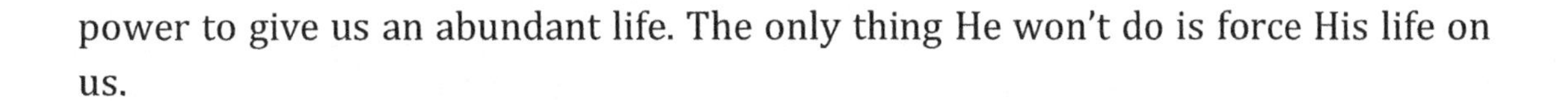

power to give us an abundant life. The only thing He won't do is force His life on us.

Why do you think God doesn't *make* us obey Him?

God wants us to choose to walk with Him and follow Him. But we still live in a fallen world and with a sinful nature. He gives us the freedom to choose a better life.

Read Colossians 3:1-17. Write a summary of what you just read:

One more thing: how do we get the power to live this life of holiness? Read John 15:1-8. What is this passage about?

Now look at Romans 12:1-2. We have to change the way we think. We have spent our lives being immersed in the world's way of thinking, which often is contradictory to God and His ways. So we need to renew our minds in the Word. We do this through changing what we read, see, listen to, and think about on a daily basis. Why? Well, what does the world have to offer you that is better than what God has to offer? Sure, you may think that our culture seems more fun and exciting. Sin is pleasurable for a time. But then we always have to pay in the end. And pay, we will.

Satan's deception is this: to get you to think that what he and the world offer is better than what God offers. Look at this list below and circle the one in each pair that you think is better.

Love or hate?

Light or darkness?

Death or life?

Good or evil?

Peace or contention?

Faith or doubt?

Sorrow or joy?

Holiness or sin?

Friend or foe?

Curse or blessing?

The truth is that all sin comes with a price. The ultimate price is death. Jesus paid that price and gave us life. But the consequences of sin in this life are pain and separation from God. Nothing separates us from His *love* for us (Romans 8:38-39), but sin will separate us from *fellowship* with Him. Confession opens the door for fellowship, and walking in holiness keeps it open so that we can enjoy the life He died to give us.

Read John 10:10. Who is the thief?

What did Jesus come to give us?

That abundant life comes through seeking God, following Jesus, walking in the Spirit.

Abundant life. Why seek anything less? Write a prayer to God now asking Him to help you walk in the Spirit. Use Romans 8:1-17 as a guide.

WEEKEND DEVO:
GOD'S PROVISION IN RELATIONSHIP

Maybe you would like a cup of tea before we get started? Okay, let's just sit here with the Lord for a few minutes. He wants to minister truth to your soul today—not religious tradition or expectations. Just let Him speak to your heart and touch you at the level of your emotions. It's okay. No, we can't live every day by what we feel, but God gave you those emotions, and He made you in His image. It's okay to feel something every now and then, friend.

Feel free to put on some soft worship music in the background while we chat.

Now, remember last week when we talked about the Song of Solomon? Solomon wrote this book, inspired by the Spirit of God, as a beautiful illustration of the relationship between a man and a woman who are passionately in love with one another. And Jesus said ALL the Scriptures concern Him. So, go right ahead and put yourself in there as the beloved, because that's who you are in this love story. And Jesus is your King.

Read chapter one. I'll wait for you.

That probably felt a little weird to you at first, but I want you to ask the Holy Spirit to reveal to your heart what these words speak about your relationship with Jesus. Let me help you understand some of it as it was interpreted by the Jews for thousands of years.

Mike Bickle of the International House of Prayer said this: "The theme of the Song of Solomon is the Bride's spiritual journey to be drawn near to Jesus in intimacy and then to run in deep partnership with Him in ministry."[viii]

Here's the first part of the Song of Solomon, chapter one. Each section begins with a label that tells who is speaking. The first section begins with the Beloved.

Beloved (That's you).

"Let him kiss me with the kisses of his mouth—for your love is more delightful than wine. Pleasing is the fragrance of your perfumes; your name is like perfume poured out. No wonder the maidens love you! Take me away with you—let us hurry! Let the king bring me into his chambers" (1:1-4).

For 3000 years, the Jews have understood the "kisses of his mouth" to be the kiss of the Torah.[ix] The Torah is the Jewish Scriptures, or the first five books of the Bible. Deuteronomy 8:3 reads that "man does not live on bread alone but on every word that comes from the mouth of the Lord." So when we read this verse, we are saying, "Lord, kiss me with Your Word. Let it touch my lips as a token of your love for me. Let me love you and desire you with all my heart."

In Matthew 22:37, Jesus repeated Deuteronomy 6 in giving us the greatest commandment: "Love the Lord your God with all your heart and with all your soul and with all your mind." That's all of you, friend. That's intimate.

The Song goes on to say that His name is like a beautiful fragrance to us, sweet and pleasant. Then in verse four we read the cry of our hearts: that Jesus would take us into His chamber, the secret place where we can be alone with Him. Because of the shed blood of Jesus on Calvary's cross, we have been invited into the holy of holies, the secret place of God's very presence.

This is what I believe is missing in so many Christian lives today. We have the head knowledge of Who Jesus is, but we are missing out on the glory of being in His presence and communing with Him on a regular basis—the very heart of who we are. Jesus paid a great price for us to have this privilege. The saints of old never "received what had been promised" while they were on this earth, but that's what they believed God for (Hebrews 11:39).

This secret place is what many call their quiet time—time they have set aside daily to spend with the Lord, to seek His face, to worship Him, to cry out to Him in prayer, to feed on His Word, to confess sins and come clean before Him. This isn't just a five-minute devotion. It's delighting in the Lord.

"Dark am I, yet lovely, O daughters of Jerusalem . . ." (1:5).

This verse describes what Mike Bickle calls the "paradox of grace."[x] We are dark with sin and yet lovely to God. Just as our children can sin, and yet we still love them, our hearts can sometimes be dark, but that never separates us from God's love.

"The heart is deceitful above all things and beyond cure" (Jeremiah 17:9).

"No, in all these things we are more than conquerors through him who loved us. For I am convinced that neither death nor life, neither angels nor demons, neither the present nor the future, nor any powers, neither height nor depth, nor anything else in all creation, will be able to separate us from the love of God that is in Christ Jesus our Lord" (Romans 8:37-39).

This truth is what brings us to God when we sin. Just as a child who knows the unconditional love of a parent will come to the parent when he has done wrong, our confidence in His love is what brings us to Him in repentance. As we dive deeper into the Song of Solomon, you will begin to see the beauty of the love relationship that God has called us to through His Son.

"How beautiful you are, my darling! Oh, how beautiful! Your eyes are doves" (1:15). Yes, that is how Jesus sees you--so beautiful that He was willing to lay down His life for you. Won't you run to Him today? Run into His strong arms and tell Him how much you love Him. Confess the darkness in your heart and let Him make you clean.

You will never be more alive than when you begin to seek Jesus every single day. Find the time that works best for you—early morning before you begin your day is usually the best time. It may seem like a sacrifice at first to rise early, but soon you will begin to anticipate this time with the Lord. Spend time praying, reading the Word, confessing your sins, and worshiping the Lord.

His kisses are truth for your soul. His fragrance is peace for your spirit. His gaze sees past your sin and straight to your sincerity and your desire to know Him more. And He loves what He sees. His love is a well that never runs dry. Drink deeply, my friend.

WEEK 4

God's Purpose in Relationship

“. . . AND ON THIS ROCK I WILL BUILD MY CHURCH, AND THE GATES OF HADES WILL NOT PREVAIL AGAINST IT.”

MATTHEW 16:18

4.1—TO WORSHIP JESUS

Now that we are clear on the difference between religion and relationship, you may be wondering, "Where does church fit into all of this?" We are called to a saving relationship with Jesus Christ, not just church membership. But the church is important. The church is the body of Christ, which means it consists of all believers in the world. It is not a building or place of worship.

When I first came to a relationship with Christ, I attended the church my grandmother went to in my small town. At just the right time, God sent a wonderful young pastor and his beautiful wife to that church. They took me under their wing and discipled me.

I'm not sure I would have survived the initial months of my salvation had it not been for God using this couple to help me. Many times I tried to slide back into the old habits of my previous lifestyle. My change wasn't automatic. I had so much to overcome, and I needed support.

This week, we are going to look at God's purpose in relationship, which is to live our relationship with Him in community. But first, let's read a few verses about the church.

Read these verses about the church and jot down what they mean to you:

Matthew 16:18

Ephesians 5:23

Colossians 1:18-20

We see here that Jesus established the church on Peter's confession and faith that He is the Christ. Jesus is the Head of the church and we are the body of Christ. For those who struggle with their identity, these Scriptures give us a great understanding of what our purpose is within the kingdom of God.

We were first and foremost created to worship God, and the Church provides a way for us to do that corporately.

Unity comes when we worship the same God in the same Spirit.

Obviously, I can love God without going to church. To be honest, worship should begin at home in our private, one-on-one relationship with God. But there is something special about coming together to worship with other believers. It's where we draw strength and a spirit of oneness. Unity comes when we worship the same God in the same Spirit. That unity brings blessings and anointing (Psalm 133).

Let's look at some verses about worship and take some notes.

Psalm 95:1-7

Psalm 100

Worship is about humbling ourselves before God, coming into His presence, and acknowledging Him as Lord over our lives. It's allowing our spirit to connect with God's Spirit. Worship is about singing, praising, bowing, thanking, praying, and loving on our awesome God. We can do that alone, but there is power when we do it as a church.

The size of the church doesn't matter. Matthew 18:20 says "For where two or three come together in my name, there am I with them." What does matter is that we love God and love each other.

Look at this passage and jot down what it says: Matthew 22:34-40.

Worship is all about loving God with all our hearts, and when we truly do that, we will also love each other. The early church was a great example for us to see what God intended for the church.

Read this passage and write what stands out to you: Acts 2:42-47.

Remember what Jesus said: The gates of hell will not be able to prevail against His church. I believe that Satan cannot prevail against a body of believers who are focused on worshiping God together as one. So it's not about religion and traditions and rules and regulations. The church is about a body of believers who know and love Jesus coming together to worship His greatness.

Find a church where you can worship Him freely and feel His presence and hear His voice. The right church is essential to understanding the role of the church in relationship and not religion. But remember, every church is made up of people—sinners saved by grace. Keep your eyes on Jesus, the Head of the Church.

Seek Him and worship Him on your own, before you go to church. Let your worship time at church just be a continuation of your private worship; then you will really begin to understand God's purpose for you in worship and as part of the Body of Christ.

4.2—TO GROW IN JESUS

When we surrender our lives to Jesus Christ, we are not automatically downloaded with a biblical worldview, but we are filled with the Spirit. His Spirit will lead us and teach us so that we can grow in our relationship and in our understanding of the Lord and His ways. Part of our purpose as believers and as the church is to grow in discipleship.

So how do we define the word *disciple?* A disciple is a fully-devoted follower or learner. Part of the role of the church is to train and make disciples for Jesus. That's what my pastor and his wife did for me. They didn't just teach the Word. They lived it in front of me.

Today we are going to study what it means to be a disciple. Let's look at some Scriptures that speak to this important aspect of knowing Jesus. Read the following and jot down your thoughts on each one.

John 8:31-32

1 Corinthians 3:1-2

Colossians 1:9-14

Hebrews 5:12-14

1 Peter 2:2-3

2 Peter 3:18

Let's think about what God's Word is teaching us. Once we come to know Jesus, it is important for us to spend time with Him daily, praying and reading His Word. This daily quiet time is the first and most important way that we grow as His disciples. To follow Jesus we need to think as He thinks. The more we study God's Word, the more we will understand His ways. We can't wait on someone else to feed us the Word; we need to open the Word and feed ourselves.

Another way we grow as disciples is through the teaching of the church, which can take place in a variety of ways, beginning with the preaching of the Word. God anoints pastors to preach His Word so we as disciples can understand the Word, follow the Word, apply it to our lives, and live in a way that pleases God. Preachers of the Word of God have a heavy responsibility to seek God and to speak the words He tells them to speak. Many times I hear people say they don't go to church because it's boring or they don't understand it. But I believe that if one is truly saved, the Holy Spirit will open her mind and give her understanding of His Word. If we know Jesus, then we will want to know more of Him. We will hunger and thirst for righteousness.

One process that helps me is to take notes. If you are prone to let your mind wander during church, start taking notes. Take your Bible to church, of course, but also take a hi-lighter, a pen, and a notebook. Focus on the pastor and listen attentively. Take notes and look for ways that you can apply the message to your own life. That active participation will help you grow as His disciple.

Another important aspect of discipleship is Bible study, which often works best in small groups. It may be a Sunday school class or a small group study, but this time is an opportunity to study particular passages of Scripture and discuss them. It will allow you to ask questions and talk about the answers. Bible study is important to our growth as Christians.

Last, it is important to have someone who is actively discipling you and helping you to grow. Paul was a mentor to Timothy, discipling Him in the Word. He encouraged, supported, instructed, and corrected him. Paul taught Timothy how to be a good soldier of Christ, and he set a good example for Timothy to follow. At some point, God will use us to disciple someone else. That process demonstrates the beauty of the Body of Christ.

Where are you in the growing process? Are you still on the milk or are you eating solid food? Are you being discipled or are you discipling someone else? We never "arrive" in our relationship with the Lord. There is always room to grow and to learn more about God. That's one of the joys of getting to know the Lord.

Think about your relationship with Jesus. Where are you on this continuum? Put an x on the line that represents your growth as a disciple of Jesus.

newborn toddler learning growing teaching maturing→

The church gives us a safe place to grow in our relationship with the Lord, but it is not a substitute or a crutch. We are responsible for our own growth. Part of God's purpose for us in relationship is th we grow and mature so that we ar able to teach and encourage others.

Our part is to go with a hunger and thirst for God...

Are you in a mentoring relationsh with someone right now, either as th mentor or as the mentee?

God calls each of us to a personal relationship with Him, and the church is vital to helping us grow in that relationship. Our part is to go with a hunger and thirst for God: to show up, to participate, and to look for ways that we can help someone else grow as well.

Remember Acts 2:42. "They devoted themselves to the apostles' teaching . . ."

So they could grow.

4.3—TO DO LIFE TOGETHER

God calls us into a personal, intimate relationship with Him. He's not looking for outward, religious rituals, but for our hearts to be changed inwardly. Worship comes from the heart—loving the Lord who has set us free and expressing that love through our lives. Yes, that can be done without going to church, but today we will look at another purpose for church, and that is fellowship.

There are many reasons we should go to church, but, technically, all the others can be accomplished without stepping foot inside a church building. By definition, fellowship cannot. Fellowship is the coming together of a group of people to interact with one another. It simply cannot be done alone.

We will look primarily at one passage today: Hebrews 10:24-25. Copy it here:

The NIV Study Bible note says, "The Greek word translated 'give up' speaks of desertion and abandonment."[xi] These verses were written to Christians who had stopped going to church.

So why do you believe it is so important to keep meeting together?

What do you think would happen if a person were saved and began going to church, and then for some reason decided to stop going? She still plans to follow Christ, but she is going to serve Him alone at home.

Let me give you an analogy. Have you ever cooked on a charcoal grill? What happens to the briquettes when you pile them in a big pyramid and then light it?

What would happen if you took one charcoal briquette out of the fire and set it aside by itself?

You're right! It will quickly burn out, which is what happens when we are not in fellowship with other believers. We have no one to hold us accountable, and it is much easier to slide back into a sinful lifestyle. We lose our passion for Jesus. We have no one with which to share our sorrows or our victories.

Read 1 Corinthians 12:12-26. The body is the church. When we are baptized into membership with a local church (verse 13), we become one body. Every part of that body is needed for the body to be complete. I am needed. You are needed. Each part should have equal concern for the other and suffer with one another and rejoice with one another (verses 25-26).

Does that sound like religion? No! But this is what the Bible teaches. We have to let go of traditions of men that have nothing to do with the Word of God and hold to those things that are biblical. For this reason, we should not give up meeting together. The church is so important. Jesus needs each one of us working together to do our part.

Let's look again at the early church when they first began to meet together after Jesus went back to heaven. Read Acts 2:42.

Name the four things the early church was devoted to:

Teaching, fellowship, eating together, and prayer—four things that sound like a lot of fun to me! I hope it is clear to you that they spent time together in fellowship. In fact, they were devoted to it. They seemed to enjoy it, too. Look at verses 46 and 47. They met together every day and ate together with *glad and sincere hearts.* They were praising God (worship) and enjoying the favor of all the people (fellowship). This description doesn't sound like stuffy religion to me. No, that is what they had just been set free from!

Fellowship is all about doing life together.

Fellowship is all about doing life together. We need each other for encouragement. When life throws difficult circumstances our way, there is nothing like having a church family to walk through them with us. We celebrate with one another and we grieve with one another. We worship together with love for the same God. We pray together for one another; we comfort one another; and, yes, sometimes we warn one another if we see someone falling into sin.

Read Galatians 6:1-2 and jot down what it speaks to you.

The Greek word used for restore means to "set bones, mend nets, or bring factions together."[xii] This word is not referring to gossip, condemnation, or judgment. Restoring is about bringing healing—not pain. We see here another example of our call to be the Body of Christ, to be used to guide and encourage one another to follow Him. I don't know about you, but I need people in my life who will lovingly help me stay on the right track.

I want you to take a few minutes and journal your thoughts about your current experience with church (or lack of). What problems have you encountered with church fellowship? What is Jesus saying to you today?

4.4—TO HELP OTHERS

Today we will look at another purpose for the church: ministry. This purpose is about how we treat one another within the Body of Christ and seek to meet needs around us—loving each other. Let's look at a few Scriptures about ministry.

We will start with the passage in Acts that we looked at yesterday.

> Read Acts 2:43-45. What wonders and miraculous signs do you think the apostles were doing?

> Why do you think they had everything in common and were willing to sell their possessions and give to anyone among them who had a need?

A friend of mine likes to call this concept "body ministry." We know that God has called us to give to the poor and help widows and orphans. We see churches with soup kitchens and clothes closets. We hear of foreign and domestic missions that rebuild homes and schools, provide food, clean water, clothing, etc. These are all examples of ministry to those in need.

But I believe that the role of the church in ministry is to meet the needs of the believers within the church. Sure, there is nothing wrong with ministry to the lost as long as it leads to the sharing of the gospel so that their greatest need (salvation) is met. When Jesus fed the five thousand or healed the sick, he was preparing their hearts for the gospel. We are called to do this type of ministry as a church, but I consider that evangelism, which we will talk about tomorrow.

Today, I want us to think about needs within the body. Christians still face sickness, loneliness, depression, loss, grief, struggles, financial problems, marriage and family difficulties. Not because God doesn't satisfy—He does! Not because God doesn't care—He does! Only because we live in a fallen world full of sin and darkness. Salvation changes us, but not our circumstances. We can be fulfilled and peaceful and joyful, even in the midst of the dark times we go through. But during those times, the church comes in to offer support.

What are some ways you think the church can help when someone goes through difficulties?

That's what the Body of Christ is all about. We are His hands and feet and voice and arms to offer comfort when a brother or sister is struggling.

Read these Scriptures and jot down what they mean to you.

Romans 12:9-16

2 Corinthians 1:3-7

Body ministry is all about forgetting our own needs and giving ourselves to meet the needs of others. What a blessing to be part of the church! We have the opportunity to make a difference in someone else's life through a phone call, a card, a hug, or a meal. Our ministry may be praying for another believer or just sitting and listening to their problems without talking about our own. We may be led to give financially to help someone through a hard time. Ministry is varied and complex, but as part of a church body, we have many opportunities to take part.

Today, most churches have ministries for children, youth, seniors, sick, shut-ins, and the bereaved. There are usually opportunities to sing in a choir, clean the church, mow the grass, teach a class, fold a bulletin, usher, or greet. All of these are opportunities to serve God while ministering to others in the Body of Christ. Everyone should be able to find a place to serve.

Body ministry is all about forgetting our own needs and giving ourselves to meet the needs of others.

But the most important ministry we can do is just to find somebody to love and encourage. That's when we are most like Christ. Who does God want you to reach out to today?

4.5—TO GO AND TELL

As we continue to look at the purpose of church, I want you to remember one thing: I'm not talking about religion. There are things that God has called us to do as a church, the Body of Christ. But what sets Christianity apart from religion is that we do these things out of our love for Him, not to earn His favor or to earn salvation.

Read Ephesians 2:8-10. We are saved by __________ through __________, not by __________. But we were created in Christ Jesus to do ________ ________. What are those good works we were created to do?

Well, yesterday we looked at many ways that we can serve and minister to those around us, but today I want us to look at the main task God has given us.

Read again the Great Commission in Matthew 28:18-20. These were Jesus' last instructions to His disciples. As His followers, we are now His disciples, so this commission is ours as well. Jesus said we are to go and make _____________. There is no more important task God has given us than to share His love and His truth with others.

We share the gospel with others, which is called evangelism, not because we are trying to earn favor with God, but because we want others to have the freedom from sin and eternal life that we have.

Read the following Scriptures and jot down what you get from each one.

Romans 1:16

Acts 5:42 (Remember Acts describes the acts of the early church.)

So how do we "evangelize" or share the gospel with others? There are many answers to that question, but we will keep it simple and look at two ways. One is lifestyle evangelism. This is living a consistent Christian life that is a witness to those around us. When I became a Christian, my family did not know the Lord. I had a pastor who taught me to "love them until they ask you 'Why?'" In other words, if we will consistently love others sincerely, they will see a difference in our lives.

Read 2 Corinthians 5:17. When we are in Christ, or saved, we are a

_______________ _______________

This verse means that the Holy Spirit comes to live inside us and change us. As we begin to change, others will see the love of God in us. If we will consistently show them radical love, even when they don't deserve it, they will eventually ask us "Why?"

As we begin to change, others will see the love of God in us.

People will want to know why we are different. That question gives us the perfect opportunity to tell them about Jesus and what He has done in our lives.

Another way to share the Gospel is sometimes called "door-to-door" evangelism, which is when we go out and share the Gospel with people that we are not in contact with on a day-to-day basis. In John chapter 4, which we studied earlier, we read about the woman that met Jesus at the well. She left the well and went back into town and told everyone what Jesus had done for her. John 4:39 says that many in her town came to believe in Jesus because of her testimony.

In this type of evangelism we share our testimony of what Jesus has done in our lives. Then we can share with them how to receive Christ as their Lord. We don't have to be preachers or evangelists to do this. If we have received Christ, then we know how to tell someone else how she can receive Christ.

This can be done door-to-door or in many different contexts, such as community outreach and missions. The bottom line is that we should always live a consistent Christian life and be prepared to tell others what Jesus has done in us.

Don't feel that you have to be perfect to live a consistent Christian life. We just have to be real. When we sin, we need to confess it and apologize to those who witnessed it. Lost people will respect us when they see that we are real, rather than if we pretend to be perfect. We strive to live each day for Jesus and own up to our mistakes when we fall short.

Read 1 Peter 3:15-16 and copy it here:

In this Scripture, we are told to always be ready to share the gospel. In the Acts 5:42 verse, we see the early church doing evangelism together. Either way, our hearts should burn for others to have the freedom in Christ that we have. That burden for the lost will come with prayer. As we begin to pray for lost people by name, the Holy Spirit will work in their hearts to help them see the truth.

Our church family is important to us in this context because we can pray together for unbelievers. We can do outreach together, such as soup kitchens, clothes closets, mission trips, community vbs (vacation Bible school). The opportunities are endless. And as we face opposition from the enemy in these times of outreach, we have each other for support and encouragement to not grow weary and give up.

So whether you are sharing your faith with a neighbor, being kind and patient at the grocery store, or serving in a foreign mission field, the goal is the same. We use whatever gifts and resources we have to tell others about Christ. He has given us a new life in Him—changed us from the inside out.

We're surrounded by people who need to know that He can change them, too.

WEEKEND DEVO: GOD'S PURPOSE IN RELATIONSHIP

Well, here we are at the end of another week of Bible study and the end of our first section, Inside Out. I pray that by now you know and understand what it means to have a personal relationship with God and allow Him to change you from the inside out.

We don't have to settle for cold, stale religion or church traditions apart from the Spirit. We can have all that Jesus died to give us—abundant life! So let's talk a little bit today what that looks like in the church. Get settled in your cozy spot and let's chat.

I know that many of you have been hurt in church. Some of you are Christians, but you no longer attend a church. I get it. Really, I do. Church is hard. We have to deal with so many obstacles from the enemy, overwhelming ministry obligations, conflict among members, and sometimes we just want to give it all up and stay home.

I've been there. But I want you to know today that God intended the church to be a place to share your love for Him and service for Him with other believers. Church on this side of eternity will never be perfect. But it can be better than what some of you have experienced. It all starts within us.

Let's go back to the Song of Solomon, our love story with the Savior.

"Dark am I, yet lovely, O Daughters of Jerusalem, dark like the tents of Kedar, like the tent curtains of Solomon. Do not stare at me because I am dark, because I am darkened by the sun. My mother's sons were angry with me and made me take care of the vineyards; my own vineyard I have neglected" (Song of Solomon 1:5-6).

Remember the speaker here is the maiden, loved by the King, expressing her anguish over the sin in her own heart. She knows that she is still lovely to her

King, but she feels ashamed because of those who stare at her. The maiden is in a spiritual crisis, feeling shame and rejection from others.

Have you ever been there?

Mike Bickle shares that within the Body of Christ, we often refer to one another as brothers and sisters in the Lord. Paul even referenced the leaders in the church metaphorically as caring for the body as a mother cares for her children (1 Thessalonians 2:7). Bickle teaches that one spiritual application that can be made here in Song of Solomon is that the maiden is experiencing spiritual burnout in the church. She has been burdened with the care of the vineyard (ministry), but has failed to tend to her own personal relationship with the Lord, which has led to sin, shame, and rejection.[xiii]

Her pressures, sin, and confusion have brought the maiden to a place of emotional and perhaps even spiritual distance from those who now stare at her and perhaps gossip behind her back. Like so many others in the church, she has fallen prey to the yoke of religion—that service without surrender, work without worship, giving without growing.

"Tell me, you whom I love, where you graze your flock and where you rest your sheep at midday. Why should I be like a veiled woman beside the flocks of your friends?" (Song of Solomon 1:7).

She is longing to once again be in His presence, to find rest at His feet, to be fed by His Word. The maiden no longer wants to worship at a distance, veiled from the King's presence. She no longer wants to feel separated from the others in the flock. So she cries out to the King, whom she loves, to show her how to find her way back.

"If you do not know, most beautiful of women, follow the tracks of the sheep and graze your young goats by the tents of the shepherds" (Song of Solomon 1:8).

The King answers her, first, by calling her "most beautiful of women." In other words, He still sees her as beautiful. Even when we fail Him, God sees us in light of His Son. Our sins are covered in the blood. We are His, and we are beautiful to Him.

Second, he tells her to follow the tracks or footsteps of the sheep. He wants her to stay committed to the flock or the church, to not run away because of their behavior or attitudes, to stay committed for His sake.

Third, she is to continue to graze or feed her flock of goats. Whatever people are under the influence of her ministry, she is called to continue to serve them, to not neglect or give up the work He has called her to do.

And fourth, he encourages her to stay under the "tents of the shepherds" or the authority of the church leaders.[xiv]

Beloved, I know that church can be so difficult, but I truly believe that if we will seek Jesus our King, first and foremost, and not neglect our personal relationship with Him, then when those difficult times come, He will gently lead us through them. He will give us the words to say or not to say. He will lead us into how much ministry to take on or not take on. He will lead us to stay and serve where we are, or He will lead us to the fellowship of believers that He wants us to serve with.

Many of the problems we face in church are because we don't seek Him first, and we end up like the beloved in this beautiful story. But rest assured, the King's love for her never wavered for a second. Neither does His love for you.

When we are truly changed from the inside out, we will experience this love that outweighs people's opinions, arguments, preferences, or rejection. We will be secure in our relationship with Jesus so that even if church does become a place that isn't what we hoped it would be, our love for God can still grow and thrive because it doesn't depend on religion.

And out of our personal relationship with the King, we can shine.

"Do everything without complaining or arguing, so that you may become blameless and pure, children of God without fault in a crooked and depraved generation, in which you shine like stars in the universe" (Philippians 2:14-15).

PART 2

INSIDE OUT:

The Culture vs. The Kingdom

UPSIDE DOWN:
THE CULTURE VS. THE KINGDOM

In this second part of the Bible study we will look at another dichotomy—today's culture as opposed to Christ's kingdom. Once we enter into God's Kingdom, we are put at odds with our culture. Let's first look at the culture of Jesus' day.

Jesus arrived on the scene somewhere between 6 and 4 B.C. during the reign of the Roman Empire and the local jurisdiction of Herod the Great. The people of Israel were left scattered, having been swept up in a succession of empires from Assyria to Rome.

Prior to the takeover of Rome, the Persians and the Greeks had allowed the Jews to carry out their religious observances without interference. By the time of Rome, the Jews were being persecuted and oppressed, and the area which had become known as Judea was ruled locally by procurators appointed by the Roman Emperors.

The Jews had become divided into several groups—the Sadducees, Pharisees, Essenes, Zealots, and the common people. I want to look briefly at each group and how they contributed to the culture of the day.

The Sadducees were the aristocrats of the Jews. They were a materialistic group who tended to hold to the status quo and political correctness. They controlled the high priesthood and rejected any doctrine not found in the Torah.

The Pharisees were a very religious and legalistic group, holding, not only to the Torah, but also to the oral traditions and their own reinterpretations of the Law in light of the culture of their day.

The Essenes were a separatist group who saw the current temple worship as corrupt. They were very devoted to the Law and sought to separate from their culture altogether.

The Zealots were a religious and political movement who opposed the oppression and taxation of the Romans and sought to bring reform to the current political environment.[xv]

So basically, by the time Jesus the Messiah arrived on the scene, the Jews were in the midst of political, social, and religious disunity. In addition to these groups were the common people, who were just trying to survive this oppressive climate, and the Romans, who were dominating the known world.

Sound familiar? King Solomon once said, "There is nothing new under the sun," (Ecclesiastes 1:9) and how right he was. Two thousand years later, we still see divisions within the Church, lost people who want nothing to do with the Church, and governments that are corrupt and oppressive.

By studying Jesus' reaction to His culture, we can learn how to respond to our culture in a time that is confusing and often volatile. Too often we react and respond to our world out of traditionally-held belief systems or self-preservation, rather than seeking God's direction in His Word.

If we are to fulfill God's call to be salt and light, we need to understand what that call means. So join me for three more weeks as we look at the culture of our world versus the Kingdom of our God.

WEEK 5

The Kingdom is Upon You

**“JESUS SAID,
‘MY KINGDOM
IS NOT OF
THIS WORLD.’”**

JOHN 18:36

5.1—THE KINGDOM HAS A KING

Let me lay a little background for us as we dive into an understanding of the Kingdom of God. First, the nation of Israel had not existed independently for over 600 years. Israel—the Jews, God's chosen people—had not been a united nation since the time of King Solomon, after whose reign the nation split into the Northern and Southern Kingdoms before falling prey to large empires.

Second, no prophets had spoken in 400 years, since the prophecy of Malachi. The books of Ezra, Nehemiah, and Ezra are the last historically; the books of Haggai, Zechariah, and Malachi are the last prophetically. These books cover the period of history after the return of a remnant of Jews to rebuild the temple, but Israel was still not independent—they were subject to the empires that ruled them.

Let's look at what the "kingdom of God" refers to according to Bible scholar Henrietta Mears in *What the Bible Is All About:*

The kingdom of heaven is also called the 'kingdom of God.' It means God's rule in the lives of His chosen people and His creation. In the Old Testament, the people were the Israelites. In the New Testament and now, the people in God's kingdom are those who believe in and follow the Lord Jesus Christ. When Jesus comes again, then God's kingdom will become visible to all people.[xvi]

The Gospel of Matthew was written by Matthew, the tax collector whom Jesus called to follow Him. Matthew wrote his gospel primarily to the Jews to prove that Jesus was the fulfillment of the prophets and the King who was to come. He used the expressions "kingdom of heaven" or "kingdom of God" over fifty times.

Read Matthew 1:1-17. In verse 17, whom does Matthew use to show the division of time leading up to Jesus' birth?

Now read the following passages and jot down what you see regarding the offspring and lineage of King David.

2 Samuel 7:11-16

Isaiah 9:6-7

Jeremiah 23:5-6

Just think: after 400 years of silence, Matthew declared that the prophesied One who would reign over Israel (and all of the world) had come. Read Matthew 1:18-25. Did you notice Matthew stressed that Joseph was a descendant of David and that Jesus was the fulfillment of the prophecies of Isaiah?

Let's read chapter two. Matthew begins with the account of the Magi who came to worship the One who was born "king of the Jews."

Why did that anger King Herod?

King Herod was a non-Jew appointed by the Roman government to "rule" over Judea, the name used to refer to the southern part of Israel at that time. He was basically a puppet of Rome, allowed to rule over the Jews, but with no power other than what Rome allowed. He was a murderer who lived lavishly at the expense of the Jewish people. In God's eyes, he was certainly not king over the Jews, and Matthew takes care to point out that Jesus was the true King.

Not only did Matthew believe that Jesus was the prophesied and coming King, but so did many people of His day.

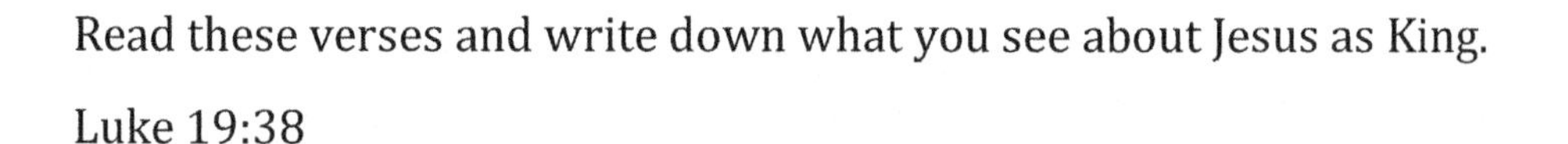

Read these verses and write down what you see about Jesus as King.

Luke 19:38

John 1:43-51

John 12:12-13

So, what about Jesus? Did He claim to be a king? Check these verses out:

Matthew 27:11

Luke 23:1-3

Yes, Jesus is the King. He not only admitted He was King of the Jews, and therefore, the fulfillment of the Scriptures that promised a King Who would reign forever; He also declared that the kingdom of God had come. We have learned what it means to have a personal relationship with the King. Over the next few weeks we will learn what it means to live within His kingdom—a kingdom that is contrary to the culture in which we live.

You see, the kingdom of God was introduced through Christ as a present reality but also as a future hope. The kingdom of God was upon them then, and it is upon us today. We have a choice to live in the fullness of the kingdom even now, and yet we put our hope in a kingdom which is still yet to come.

The Lord Jesus Christ reigns over all creation, yet the enemy has been given free reign over earth for a limited time. That means that as part of the kingdom of God, we have become enemies of the kingdom of darkness. So how do we live amidst a culture that does not submit to His reign?

We will look at this question this week as we pursue an understanding of God's kingdom, which is within us. We live in the world, but our citizenship is with the kingdom of God. And we bow to Him only.

We live in the world, but our citizenship is with the kingdom of God.

"Therefore God exalted him to the highest place and gave him the name that is above every name, that at the name of Jesus every knee should bow, in heaven and on earth and under the earth, and every tongue confess that Jesus Christ is Lord, to the glory of God the Father" (Philippians 2:9-11).

Take a few minutes and write out a prayer to King Jesus, acknowledging His authority as your King.

5.2—THE KINGDOM HAS SUBJECTS

Yesterday, we studied the coming of Jesus as the King Whom God had said through the prophets would reign forever. Daniel prophesied that Jesus' "kingdom will be an everlasting kingdom, and all rulers will worship and obey him" (Daniel 7:27).

So just who are the subjects of this kingdom? Jesus was proclaimed as King of the Jews, so where does that leave those who are not Jews?

Read Psalm 47. Whom does this Scripture say that God reigns over?

That's right. God reigns over all the earth through His Son Jesus. So when we become believers in Jesus Christ, we become the subjects of this kingdom. Today, we are going to study what Jesus said about being a part of this kingdom. To the Jews of His day, many of these words probably came as a surprise.

Read Matthew 5:1-12. To whom was Jesus speaking?

The word *blessed* literally means "receiving God's favor, fortunate, good (in a position of favor), happy (feelings associated with receiving God's favor)."

Fill out the following chart.

Who is blessed	Why they are blessed

Compare verse three and verse ten. What do both verses say belongs to those being described?

If you had to summarize these characteristics, how would you describe the person who is part of the kingdom of God?

This description would have come as a shock to the religious people of Jesus' day. They boasted in their righteousness; Jesus said the kingdom belonged to those who were poor in spirit.

Poor in spirit means "realizing they have nothing to offer God but are in need of his free gifts."[xvii] The kingdom belongs to those who are humble enough to admit their total dependence upon God.

> Read Matthew 5:13-16. What two things did Jesus say His subjects should be?

Here in the very next breath, Jesus called His subjects to be salt and light. Salt was used for flavoring and as a preservative. He said the salt needed to stay salty and the light needed to keep shining. So even though He called us to be meek (meaning gentle, humble, and kind), He also called us to be a positive moral influence on those around us. When the persecution of verses 10-12 came, they were told to stay salty and bright.

In other words, humility and peacefulness are not excuses to hide in our corner of belief and be silent subjects of the kingdom. A city on a hill cannot be hidden. We are that city. Remember that the Jews of Jesus' day were under persecution from the Roman Empire. Jesus said they would be blessed because of this persecution, but they had to continue to shine and bring flavor to those around them.

The subjects of the kingdom of God are those who recognize their need for God, mourn over their own sin, show gentleness and kindness, hunger and thirst for righteous-ness, show mercy, have pure hearts toward God, make peace, and as a result, are persecuted and insulted by others. But they don't let the culture dictate who they are. They are happy to be in the kingdom, and they let it show.

The culture doesn't influence the kingdom. The kingdom influences its culture with salt and light.

The culture doesn't influence the kingdom. The kingdom influences its culture with salt and light.

How can we add flavor (make the kingdom palatable) and preservative (preserve the kingdom truths), even in times of persecution and false accusations?

How can we be light to the world?

If we are subjects of God's kingdom, that's what we are called to do. We can stay salty and bright because we are blessed to be in the kingdom of the One Who reigns over all the earth.

5.3—THE KINGDOM HAS LAWS

Every kingdom has laws by which the king exercises his authority. We are going to pick up right where we left off yesterday in Matthew 5, beginning in verse 17. Read through verse 20.

This passage is so important to understanding the relationship between the teachings of the Old Testament Law and the teachings of Jesus. Many people think they contradict one another or that we are no longer bound by the moral Law of the Old Testament. Neither of these thoughts is true.

Jesus said He came to (circle one)

A. explain the Law and the Prophets

B. abolish the Law and the Prophets

C. fulfill the Law and the Prophets

D. add to the Law and the Prophets

The Law and the Prophets would have referred to the entire Old Testament. I want to share a note in *The NIV Study Bible* that really explains this passage well.

> Jesus fulfilled the Law in the sense that he gave it its full meaning. He emphasized its deep, underlying principles and total commitment to it rather than mere external acknowledgment and obedience . . . Jesus is not speaking against observing all the requirements of the Law, but against hypocritical, Pharisaical legalism. Such legalism was not the keeping of all details of the Law but the hollow sham of keeping laws externally, to gain merit before God, while breaking them inwardly. It was following the letter of the Law while ignoring its spirit. Jesus repudiates the Pharisees' interpretation of the Law and their view of righteousness by works. He preaches a righteousness that comes only through faith in him and his work. In the verses that follow, he gives six examples of Pharisaical externalism.[xviii]

I really couldn't say it any better. So, let's look at those six examples.

> Read Matthew 5:21-26. According to Jesus, the spirit of the commandment to not murder is what?

> Read Matthew 5:27-30. What is the spirit of the commandment to not commit adultery?

> Read Matthew 5:31-32. What is the spirit of the laws regarding divorce?

> Read Matthew 5:33-37. What is the spirit of the law about oaths?

> Read Matthew 5:38-42. What is the spirit of the law regarding retaliation (see Exodus 21:24)? This one may require a little more study. Basically, the law was intended to be a deterrent to prevent harm. Can you think of ways the Israelites may have used this law as an excuse to exact revenge?

> Read Matthew 5:43-48. What is the spirit of the law regarding loving your neighbor?

In each of these examples, Jesus goes beyond the outward obedience to the law and gets to the heart of the matter: our inward life. To the religious leaders, outward obedience was all that mattered. To Jesus, our heart, mind, and motivation are just as important.

Now let's look at a few more verses that enlighten us about Jesus' fulfillment of the Law.

Read the following verses and jot down a few notes about each.

Romans 10:1-4

Galatians 3:21-25

Matthew 22:37-39

The Israelites were given very specific laws regarding moral living, their sacrificial system, and dietary and customary laws that set them apart as a nation. Jesus fulfilled the sacrificial laws through His death. Christians are not bound by the Israelites' dietary and customary laws (such as circumcision) because we are now set apart by the Spirit.

In Matthew 22, Jesus said that all the Law and the Prophets could be summed up by loving God and loving others. These two laws cover all of the Ten Commandments, God's moral law. Remember the first four deal with our love for God, and the last six deal with our love for others. These laws were given to the Israelites to show them God's moral requirements and their own inability to keep them. Breaking these laws makes us sinners, but obeying them doesn't save us.

We are saved through faith in Jesus, whose righteousness covers us and sets us free from the burden of a law we can't keep.

But that doesn't mean that the Kingdom of God is without moral standards. We still have laws. We still have rules. We still have a standard in God's Word that He calls us to as His followers. When we surrender our lives to Jesus, we become a new creation—changed from the inside out.

Our hearts change; our desires change; our motivations change. One of my favorite passages when I first got saved was Colossians 3:1-17. In my *NIV Study Bible*, the passage is titled "Rules for Holy Living." I love that because when you fall in love with Jesus, you walk in His love and grace, but you also desire to walk in His holiness. This passage gives us specific guidelines for how to do just that.

Read Colossians 3:1-17. Answer the following questions.

What does it mean to be raised with Christ?

What should we set our heart on?

What should we set our mind on?

What should we put to death?

What should we rid ourselves of?

What should we clothe ourselves with?

What should be worn over everything else?

Why do you think these "rules of holy living" are important for Christians if we are set free?

What is the difference between obeying these rules out of love for Christ and having a religious, legalistic attitude toward sin?

I pray that we are never content with religious rules, but that we hunger for holy living. Lord, fill our hearts and minds with Your truth and not our own.

I pray that we are never content with religious rules, but that we hunger for holy living.

5.4—THE KINGDOM IS WITHIN

Remember we learned that the kingdom of God is where He rules and reigns. It is a present reality in our lives as believers and also has a future fulfillment when Jesus returns to reign here on earth in His eternal kingdom. Today we are going to study where this kingdom is set up now.

> Read Luke 17:20-21. Where did Jesus tell them they would find the kingdom?

Remember in Matthew 23 when Jesus told the Pharisees to first clean the inside of the cup and dish, and then the outside also would be clean? He is emphasizing again that the place where God rules is where He has authority (beginning within). If the kingdom is here now, then it is only present within those who give Him authority over their lives.

> Read John 3:1-8. What did Jesus tell Nicodemus was required to see the kingdom of God?

So we are beginning to see that the kingdom of God is where God rules and reigns in our lives, having all authority; and we must be born again, changed from the inside out, to be living in this kingdom.

> Let's go back to where we left off in Matthew with chapter 6. Read 6:1-4. How should our giving to the needy be done?

Read 6:5-15. How should our praying be done?

Read 6:16-18. How should our fasting be done?

Read 6:19-24. What should we treasure most in life?

Read 6:25-34. Why do we not need to worry about material things if we are seeking the kingdom?

Write Matthew 6:33 below.

Can you see that Jesus was calling us to a kingdom that is much deeper than what the religious leaders of His day understood? The Pharisees believed that outward observance of these things made them right with God. Jesus came along and turned their understanding of the kingdom upside down. He said we needed to be surrendered from the inside out. Jesus said that He looks at our hearts and our desire to please Him. He is more interested in our "who" than our "do."

Jesus came along and turned their understanding of the kingdom upside down.

If we have to give, pray, and fast in order to be seen by others and thought well of by the church, then we are not truly in the kingdom. When we are subjects of the kingdom, we serve the King because He is worthy. We serve Him because He deserves it. We live in the kingdom because there is no place we would rather be.

Let's see who Jesus said would be thrown out of the kingdom. Read Matthew 8:5-13. At first this passage may seem troubling. Why would the subjects of the kingdom be thrown out of the kingdom? The Greek word that is translated *subjects* here literally means "son, child, descendent." The Pharisees believed that they were automatically subjects of the kingdom because they were the "sons" of Abraham. This passage is about a Gentile (a Roman centurion) who showed real faith in Jesus. The Lord is saying that this guy had true faith, while many of the Jews would be thrown out of the kingdom because they had no such faith. Wow.

The secrets of the kingdom are revealed to those who seek the kingdom and surrender to the authority of the King.

Tomorrow we are going to explore some of the parables that reveal the secrets of the kingdom, but today I want you to see one of them because it fits our study of where we find the kingdom.

Read Matthew 21:28-32. Look at the context in the previous passages. To whom is Jesus speaking?

Who did Jesus tell them were entering the kingdom of God ahead of them?

Why would Jesus say that to the religious leaders?

Read Matthew 7:15-23. Since the kingdom is within, how does Jesus say that we will be able to know who is in the kingdom and who is not?

Think about your experience with your culture. Do you have any thoughts about God that are counter to what Jesus actually taught? Are you able to recognize teachings such as that of the Pharisees which actually contradict Jesus' teachings about the kingdom?

Ask the Holy Spirit to reveal to you any traditional belief systems that do not line up with His revelation of truth in Scripture. The kingdom is within, but it will be revealed without through the fruit we bear.

5.5—THE SECRETS OF THE KINGDOM

Jesus shared the secrets of the kingdom through parables. The parables have often been called earthly stories with heavenly meanings. The Greek word translated *parable* means "an illustration that teaches in a story or extended figure of speech."[xix] So why did Jesus often teach about the kingdom in parables?

> Let's ask Him. Read Matthew13:1-23. This is the first recorded parable in the Gospels. In verse 10 the disciples asked Him why He spoke in parables. What did Jesus tell them?

First, Jesus told the disciples that they were given the secrets of the kingdom because they had the kingdom within (whoever has will be given more). Those who had rejected Him would not be able to understand because their unbelief had blinded them from truth.

Second, I believe the parables challenged those who were sincere to search deeper and seek Him more. These stories presented truths about the kingdom that oftentimes had to be prayerfully contemplated and studied as we are doing now. That searching divides the sheep from the goats.

We are going to look at a few of these parables about the kingdom of God. I pray this study will encourage you to search out more of them for yourself.

Since Jesus explained the first parable, let's go to the next one in Matthew 13:24-30. This parable actually got explained by Jesus as well, so jump down to 13:36-43.

> What does this parable teach about the kingdom of God?

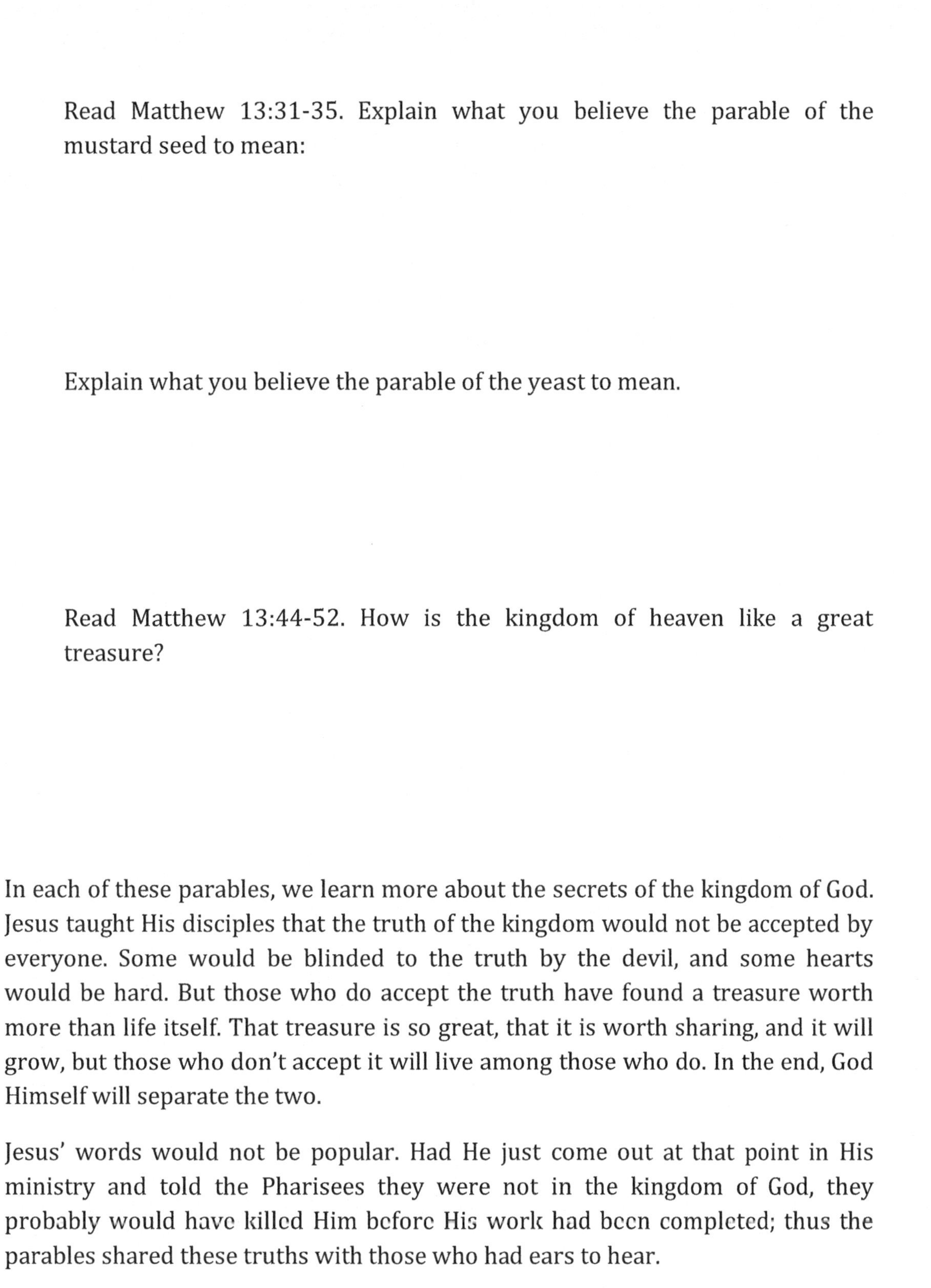

Read Matthew 13:31-35. Explain what you believe the parable of the mustard seed to mean:

Explain what you believe the parable of the yeast to mean.

Read Matthew 13:44-52. How is the kingdom of heaven like a great treasure?

In each of these parables, we learn more about the secrets of the kingdom of God. Jesus taught His disciples that the truth of the kingdom would not be accepted by everyone. Some would be blinded to the truth by the devil, and some hearts would be hard. But those who do accept the truth have found a treasure worth more than life itself. That treasure is so great, that it is worth sharing, and it will grow, but those who don't accept it will live among those who do. In the end, God Himself will separate the two.

Jesus' words would not be popular. Had He just come out at that point in His ministry and told the Pharisees they were not in the kingdom of God, they probably would have killed Him before His work had been completed; thus the parables shared these truths with those who had ears to hear.

The secrets of the kingdom of God are revealed to those who seek the kingdom and surrender to the authority of the King. And the great news is that for those of us who are born again, who believe by faith in Jesus Christ, we have a treasure worth more than anything the world has to offer.

"Therefore, since we are receiving a kingdom that cannot be shaken, let us be thankful, and so worship God acceptably with reverence and awe, for our 'God is a consuming fire'" (Hebrews 12:28-29).

WEEKEND DEVO: THE KINGDOM IS UPON YOU

I so hope and pray that you are enjoying studying God's Word as much as I am. It's time for your weekend devo—your opportunity to just sit back and listen and let God's Word minister to your heart today.

As I studied these Scriptures about the kingdom this week, I was reminded of a story in Matthew chapter twelve. Jesus healed a man who was both blind and mute because of a demonic spirit, but the Pharisees claimed He did it through power that came from Satan.

Jesus first responded to them by saying that a kingdom divided against itself would not stand. In other words, if He were driving out Satan by the power of Satan, then He would destroy Himself. Second, He asked by whose power did their people call on to drive demons out?

The Pharisees and their disciples apparently claimed to cast out demons as well, so if they believed God was working in them, why did they not believe God's power was at work in Jesus?

Then Jesus said this: "But if I drive out demons by the Spirit of God, then the kingdom of God has come upon you" (Matthew 12:28).

That was powerful! Let me tell you what Jesus was saying here. When the kingdom of God is at work, miracles happen. Jesus' ministry came with many signs and wonders. Jesus not only cast out demons, but also healed the sick, calmed the storm, walked on water, multiplied fish and bread, turned water into wine, and raised the dead.

When John the Baptist questioned whether Jesus was the Messiah or whether they should look for someone else, Jesus sent His disciples to John with this message:

> "Go back and report to John what you hear and see: The blind receive sight, the lame walk, those who have leprosy are cured, the deaf hear, the dead are raised, and the good news is preached to the poor. Blessed is the man who does not fall away on account of me" (Matthew 11:4-6).

Jesus demonstrated the power of God through all of these miracles to show that the kingdom of God had indeed come. And now that His kingdom has come, we have the opportunity to not only be a part of the kingdom, but to live out the power of the kingdom every day.

As we will see in the next two weeks, kingdom living is counter-cultural. It goes against everything for which the world stands. Jesus took our world philosophy and turned it completely upside down. What the world prizes, the kingdom resists. What the world hates, the kingdom seeks. We live and move in this world, but within the kingdom of love and God's power.

Look at these verses that teach the counter-cultural view of the kingdom.

"One man gives freely, yet gains even more; another withholds unduly, but comes to poverty" (Proverbs 11:24).

"Not by might not by power, but by my Spirit, says the Lord" (Zechariah 4:6).

"For when I am weak, then I am strong" (2 Corinthians 12:10).

"The man who loves his life will lose it, while the man who hates his life in this world will keep it for eternal life" (John 12:25).

"Bless those who persecute you; bless and do not curse" (Romans 12:14).

"Humble yourselves before the Lord, and he will lift you up" (James 4:10).

"Give and it will be given to you" (Luke 6:38).

As you can see, truth in God's kingdom is opposed to what our culture teaches.

"But God chose the foolish things of the world to shame the wise; God chose the weak things of the world to shame the strong. He chose the lowly things of this world and the despised things—and the things that are not—to nullify the things that are, so that no one may boast before him" (1 Corinthians 1:27-29).

So if we are living in the kingdom, surrendered to the King, our lives should reflect the love, humility, truth, and power of Jesus. We should be seeing miracles in our day, reflecting the power of God in our midst.

Being salt—living in a way that makes the world want what we have because it is tasty, while not compromising but rather preserving the truth of the Gospel.

Being light—shining brightly with the peace, presence, and power of Christ in our lives.

How do we live this upside-down life in our present-day culture?

By falling in love with the King, sitting at His feet, feasting at His table. The more we grow in our love for and understanding of God and His Word, the more we will be able to impact our world for Him—side by side with others who love Him, too.

Do you want to impact your world for Christ? Then start living out the power of the kingdom by seeking first His kingdom and His righteousness and by being salt and light to a world that is spoiling and fading. They won't all understand or respond to the truth. But at least they will know that the kingdom is upon them.

WEEK 6

The Kingdom Costs

“BUT SEEK FIRST THE KINGDOM AND HIS RIGHTEOUSNESS, AND ALL THESE THINGS WILL BE GIVEN TO YOU AS WELL.”

MATTHEW 6:33

6.1—COUNT THE COST

This week we will focus our study on the cost of the kingdom. Let me begin by stressing that salvation is free: Jesus totally paid the price for our sin, and when we accept that sacrifice by faith, we are saved.

"For it is by grace you have been saved, through faith—and this not from yourselves, it is the gift of God—not by works, so that no one can boast" (Ephesians 2:8-9).

Salvation is free, not earned; and yet following Jesus will cost us. In economics, we call this opportunity cost.

> "Opportunity cost refers to a benefit that a person could have received, but gave up, to take another course of action. Stated differently, an opportunity cost represents an alternative given up when a decision is made."[xx]

In other words, Jesus paid the price for our sin; we pay the price of what we give up in order to follow Him.

> Read the following Scriptures: Proverbs 4:7, 1 Corinthians 1:30, Colossians 2:2-3, and Matthew 13:45-46. According to these Scriptures, what can you conclude about the value of following Jesus?

> Do you think the opportunity cost is worth the value of the kingdom?

Let's see what some followers of Jesus gave up to follow Him.

Read Matthew 4:21-22. What did these fishermen leave behind to follow Jesus?

Read Matthew 8:18-22. What do you think Jesus was saying here about the cost of following Him?

Read Mark 8:34-37. What did Jesus say we must deny in order to follow Him?

Look at Luke 9:57-62. This is Luke's version of the account we read in Matthew 8, except Luke includes more of Jesus' words in verses 61-62. At first glance, we may think that Jesus was telling His followers that taking care of their families wasn't important, but that's not what Jesus was saying. Scholars tell us that according to Jewish custom, if the second man's father had already died, he would have been occupied with burying him right then. Instead, he wanted to wait until after his father's death to follow Jesus. In both of these situations, we see people who are giving excuses for not following Jesus right then, no matter the cost. Remember, Jesus knew their hearts. He was showing them the high cost of following Him, which meant that family would come second.

Look back at Matthew 10:34-39. Whom did Jesus say we shouldn't love more than Him?

The cost of the kingdom is high. We don't hear that preached much today, do we? We hear a lot about the love and grace and mercy of God, but we seldom hear that we may have to give up everything to follow Jesus. But isn't that what He said?

Let's look at one more passage. Turn with me to Luke 14:25-33. What do you think Jesus meant by verse 26?

His words are what we call hyperbole—extreme exaggeration used to make a point. Jesus did not literally mean that we should hate our family. That premise would go against all that He taught about love. He was saying that our love for Him should be so great that our love for family would look like hate in comparison. Jesus called us to an extreme, radical level of commitment to Him that goes far beyond even what we have for our own families.

What did Jesus say in verse 33 that we should be willing to give up for Him?

The cost of the kingdom is complete surrender. Do you know why?

Because anything less than that is not faith. Jesus has called us to surrender self, family, career, and everything else that is important to us in order to follow Him, because if we don't, we will end up putting all those things ahead of the kingdom. And the kingdom of God is something far greater. Our earthly lives, relationships, careers, hobbies, and ministries are all temporary. But the kingdom is eternal.

The cost of the kingdom is complete surrender.

Jesus calls us to surrender all we are and all we have and commit to something far beyond ourselves—something that has stood through the ages, that Satan can't conquer, and time cannot diminish.

He calls us to a kingdom that cannot be shaken and a life that cannot be called our own. As we will see later this week, few actually follow this way because it goes against everything within us, and yet it fills our deepest need.

It's the greatest love story of all time, the championship of the ages, the adventure of all eternity. Yes, the kingdom of God is worth all that we can fathom, and yet so few find it. Because the kingdom comes at a great price. Are you willing to give your all for the glory of the King? If so, tell Him now.

6.2—HIS WAY, NOT MINE

Yesterday, we took a look at the cost of the kingdom. If we truly surrender all in radical commitment to King Jesus, then it will cost us. The remainder of this week, we will look at what some of those costs are. First, the kingdom will cost us our will, our way, and our plans.

Turn first to Isaiah 55:8-9. Our thoughts are not ________________. Our ways are not ____________________. According to verse 9, whose thoughts and ways are higher?

Before we come to understand God and His ways, we often think that our way is better. But part of living in the kingdom is coming to understand God and His ways.

Read the following verses and jot down what God speaks to you through them.

2 Samuel 22:31-33

Psalm 25:9-10

Proverbs 4:11-12

Proverbs 19:21

From these few verses, what can you conclude about God's ways?

Remember that when Jesus called His disciples, He asked them to leave everything and follow Him.

Why do you think He did that?

Fishermen laid down their nets; tax collectors left the collector's booth. Some left their fathers. But do you think Jesus called people to leave the families they were supporting?

Let's read Matthew 8:14. Whose house did Jesus visit?

Peter apparently didn't walk away from responsibility to his family in order to follow Jesus, but he did leave behind his own plans and pursuits. Following Jesus simply means laying aside our way of thinking and doing and following His way. For some, that may mean a change in career, plans, and dreams. But we can rest assured that His way is the better way. When Jesus called His disciples, He sent them out with specific ministry to do. They were to follow Him and depend on Him to provide for their needs.

It's easy to think this life is our own and we have the right to do with it as we please. God will certainly let us keep that right should we choose. But being in the kingdom means that we give up the right to our own way and our own pursuits because we are following a better way.

Did you know that early Christians were sometimes called followers of the Way?

Read John 14:6. Jesus said He is the ________, ________, and ________.

Can you think of songs, slogans, and sayings that promote doing things our way and following our own dreams?

Our culture promotes the belief in self and our ability to determine our own path. God's Word tells us just the opposite. When we follow Jesus, we leave behind our old ways for His way. Even Jesus chose to follow the will of the Father.

Read these Scriptures and jot down what they speak to you.

Matthew 6:9-10

Matthew 26:39

John 6:38

The kingdom of God is about surrendering our will to the will of the Lord. Living in the kingdom means that we are choosing to lay down our plans and take up the Father's plans, no matter what that means. It may mean sacrifice. It may mean less money. It may mean not fulfilling our own dreams. But God has a better plan and a better dream for each of us.

Following Jesus is not about taking our plans and stamping God's name over the top of them. Jesus said it would involve taking up our cross. The cross was a form of execution that had been perfected by the Romans. When a man was sentenced to death on a Roman cross, his life was over. Once he took up his cross, there would be no going back. He literally walked away from his life and walked to his death. When we take up our cross, we are walking away from our old lives, and literally laying down every plan and dream we have ever had. We are walking forward to our death—death of self, sin, and our former way of life.

Following Jesus is not about taking our plans and stamping His name over the top of them.

Can we take a few minutes and ask God to search our hearts? Are there any areas that maybe we have held onto, some dreams we are still pursuing that God didn't call us to? Perhaps we have decided to follow Jesus as long as we still get to follow our career or education or family goals? The Lord wants you to know you can trust Him with your present and your future. Ask the Holy Spirit to probe the deepest areas of your soul and show you anything you have not yielded to Him.

6.3—LAST, NOT FIRST

Yesterday's lesson may have left you with some painful areas in your heart. That's okay. Let the Holy Spirit do His work and have His way. Today we are going to look at another cost of kingdom living that may be difficult to confront: our pride.

When Jesus began teaching and preaching, the religious leaders of His day thought they had the monopoly on the kingdom. Because the Israelites were God's chosen nation to whom the promise of the Messiah came, they believed they were in right standing with God, regardless of what was in their hearts.

> Read Matthew 3:1-9. What did John the Baptist tell the Pharisees was more important than being a "child of Abraham"?

Read John 8:31-47. Notice verse 31. The verse reads, "To the Jews who had believed him," but later He tells them that they do not belong to God (v. 47). Scholars say that these were probably Jews who had made a profession of faith from their mouths but did not truly believe in their hearts.

> What did Jesus tell them would set them free? Look closely at verse 31.

Obedience to God and His teachings are evidence that we truly belong to His kingdom.

In Jesus' teachings we can see that He stressed inward motivation of the heart above outward profession of faith. Religious pride and status are out the door. Obedience to God and His teachings are evidence that we truly belong to His kingdom. Many of the Jews and religious leaders believed their position as children of Abraham and their status in the religious establishment were what designated them as members of the kingdom. Jesus turned that whole belief system upside down.

Let's read some passages about those to whom Jesus said the kingdom belonged.

> Read Matthew 18:1-9 and 19:13-14. Whom did Jesus identify as the citizens of the kingdom of heaven and why?

> How do you think the religious leaders felt when they heard these words?

This religious pride didn't only affect the Pharisees and religious leaders. Jesus had to have a little talk with His disciples, too.

> Read Matthew 20:20-28. What did Jesus say was the key to becoming great?

> How do you think the disciples felt when they heard these words?

When we look at our culture today, it's sometimes easy to think that those who are "sinners" don't deserve to receive the kingdom, but we have to remember we don't deserve it either.

> Read Matthew 9:9-13. Whom did Jesus say He came to call?

These words would have greatly offended the religious leaders who truly believed that they would be the first to inherit the kingdom of God. They looked down on those who weren't part of their inner circle. But Jesus came for the last and the least, not those who believe they are first and best.

> Read Matthew 21:28-32. Write below what you believe Jesus was saying about the kingdom of God and the way of righteousness.

Jesus taught that the kingdom of God belongs to those who are willing to give up their pride and status and walk in God's ways of righteousness. Following His commands from our hearts is what God desires—not outward acts of righteousness that look good—not seeking to be the head-honcho, the boss, the one who knows it all. Jesus said if you want to be first, you need to be last. If you want to be great, you need to be a servant.

Read Mark 9:33-37. Jesus was clear about the cost of following Him. In our culture, we are told to aim for the top. Even in the church, we are sometimes encouraged to forge ahead with our plans and our pride, seeking some religious status that will earn us something in the kingdom. But that's not God's way. We need to spend time in God's Word and really listen to what the Word says.

Sometimes here in Western culture, we think we already know what it means to be a Christian. But oftentimes we are following the Westernized brand of Christianity—the comfortable, God-wants-you-to-be-happy-and-prosperous version of the Gospel that flies in the face of the red letters.

Do you want to truly know what it means to be in the kingdom? Ask the King.

6.4—CHARACTER, NOT COMFORT

I hope you have had some time to recover from the last couple of days of study. I have some really tender places in my heart that the Lord is dealing with even now. Truth hurts, but it will also set us free when we accept it. Next week when we look at the rewards of the kingdom, I pray you will agree that the costs are worth it.

Today we will look at another cost of the kingdom: our treasure. Our Western world tends to treasure stuff. We work hard to have what we have and place much value on earthly treasures. Jesus taught us what true treasure is.

Read the following Scriptures and jot down what you get from each.

Matthew 6:19-24

Matthew 6:25-34

Matthew 13:44-46

Mark 12:41-44

We Americans place a high value on our jobs, incomes, and possessions. We educate for around twenty years so that we can get high-paying salaries. After all, we have to provide for our families, right? But when I think of how much stuff we have and our children have, it's almost embarrassing—especially in light of how little so many Christians in the world have. Yet those Christians would tell you how blessed they are to be able to serve Christ and be part of His kingdom.

God cares far more about our character than our comfort. Don't get me wrong. Jesus had compassion on the helpless and harassed, and He came to bring comfort to those who mourn (Matthew 5:4), but we misunderstand what comfort means. In Western culture, we believe that means God wants us to be happy and have everything we want in life.

God cares more about our character than our comfort.

The Hebrew word for comfort literally means "to relent, repent, change one's mind."[xxi] In other words, comfort means mercy—to not give us what we deserve for our sin. Comfort means to stay God's hand of judgment and instead receive peace. Jesus had compassion and comfort for those who were lost. We think He wants us to be comfortable in life, prosperous, and wealthy, but the blessings of God are far better than that.

Think about it: would you rather have a fancy home here on earth or an eternal home in heaven? Would you rather have everything you want now for a few years or have everything you could ever dream or think of for all eternity? The problem is we think too small and too short-termed. We want it all now. And for many in the church today, we think following Jesus means He will bless us with our best life now. But our best life is yet to come.

One of the costs of the kingdom is our treasure. Jesus wants us to let go of earthly treasure and value His kingdom instead. That may mean giving up some of life's comforts in order to serve Him. Take some time today to think about what you value most in life. Is there anything that may be standing in the way of your doing the will of God in your life? How comfortable are you with the here and now? Where is your treasure?

Many years ago, I attended a Gaither conference for those interested in music ministry. I'll never forget the wise words of Gloria Gaither to a group of young people excited about singing and ministering for the Lord. She asked us to evaluate what our purpose was in ministry. Were we excited to be on a stage or behind a microphone or perhaps to even have a recording made with our name across a cd cover? Or were we passionate about the things of God that would matter for eternity—souls being saved and hearts and lives touched by God. Because our purpose for being in ministry would make all the difference in how we carried out that ministry. If our purpose was simply to make a difference for the kingdom of God, she asked, couldn't that be done within the local church without a record label or the accolades? Would we be content if that was all God ever asked us to do? Her final words to us were an admonition to ask one question about everything we do in our lives, "What is eternal about this moment?"

Let's let that answer determine our path.

6.5—NARROW, NOT WIDE

On our last day of study this week, we will look at one more cost to the kingdom: popularity. For many, the loss of popularity and good standing among men can be devastating. It used to be for me.

I was never very popular in school, so I coveted having friends and being well thought of by others. When I became a believer, I worked really hard to be accepted by others within the Christian community. But I have since come to realize that I would rather be accepted and approved of by God.

Our culture places much value on popularity—social media is evidence of that. Today's culture magnifies the thrill of getting more friends, followers, likes, and comments than the next person—especially if those responses are based on our perceived beauty (via selfie posts).

Human nature seeks to be popular. That's why we fall prey to the latest fads. Whatever the celebrities decide is the popular color, design, hairstyle, etc. is what we feel we have to have. We want to fit in. But Jesus said the kingdom way was not the popular way.

> Read Matthew 7:13-14. How many people did Jesus say would be on the "road that leads to life"?
>
> Why do you think that is?
>
> Read Matthew 9:35-38. Why are the workers few?

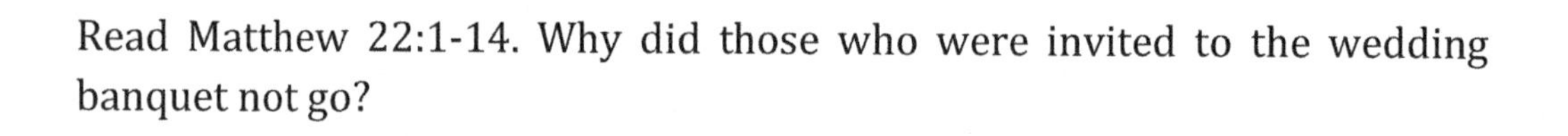

Read Matthew 22:1-14. Why did those who were invited to the wedding banquet not go?

So according to this parable, why are there only a few chosen?

If everything about kingdom living were easy (as our culture would sometimes have us believe about Christianity), then why did Jesus say that only a few would actually follow this way of living?

Read Luke 13:22-30. Why did Jesus tell them that only a few would actually be saved?

Our religious culture in America sells many books and conference tickets proclaiming that we can become Christians and live a "blessed" life. Jesus seems to be the key to life, liberty, and the pursuit of happiness. Oh, wait! That's the American dream. Yes, I believe we have confused the two.

Kingdom living is about sacrifice. One of the costs of the kingdom is giving up the thrill of popularity. Instead, we will often have to swim against the stream, be politically incorrect, and even face persecution because of our beliefs in God and His Word. Doesn't sound like a path many will take, does it?

Jesus never promised ease for those who follow Him. Read John 15:18-25 and John 16:33. We will face trouble and persecution if we choose to follow Jesus. But we are following the One who has overcome it all. The way is narrow, but it leads to life. All are offered, but few will follow. What will you choose? Why?

Jesus never promised ease for those who follow Him.

WEEKEND DEVO:
THE COST OF THE KINGDOM

Whew! That was a tough week of study. I pray that you are still hanging with me. Jesus sometimes had some tough words for His followers that were difficult to swallow. Many actually gave up on Him.

"From this time many of his disciples turned back and no longer followed him" (John 6:66).

Yeah. The rich, young ruler wasn't the only one who walked away. Why did many of Jesus' followers decide to turn back?

"On hearing it [Jesus' teaching], many of his disciples said, 'This is a hard teaching. Who can accept it?'" (John 6:60).

Many turned away from following Him because the message was hard. We don't hear much preaching on this little story in the Gospels. Instead, we live in America—Land of the Free and Home of the Brave—where Christianity is the default religion. We live in a culture in which we have watered down the gospel so that it's appealing to everyone.

But even Jesus didn't do that. He spoke truth. The gospel is appealing on its own, but not because it's easy.

We learned this week that walking in the kingdom means that we give up our rights to self—our way, our pride, our comfort, our popularity. We walk away from our former way of living and we take a new path—one that leads to life and is characterized, not by sin or by self-righteousness, but by the Spirit of God.

So why would any of us willingly give up the right to rule on our own throne and let a God we've never seen rule over us instead?

Because of Jesus' love and sacrifice for us. Period.

"For God so loved the world that he gave his one and only Son, that whoever believes in him shall not perish but have eternal life. For God did not send his Son into the world to condemn the world, but to save the world through him" (John 3:16-17).

"But God demonstrates his own love for us in this: While we were still sinners, Christ died for us" (Romans 5:8).

"For the wages of sin is death, but the gift of God is eternal life in Christ Jesus our Lord" (Romans 6:23).

"In him we have redemption through his blood, the forgiveness of sins, in accordance with the riches of God's grace that he lavished on us with all wisdom and understanding" (Ephesians 1:7-8).

"He forgave us all our sins, having canceled the written code, with its regulations, that was against us and that stood opposed to us; he took it away, nailing it to the cross" (Colossians 2:13b-14).

"This is love: not that we loved God, but that he loved us and sent his Son as an atoning sacrifice for our sins" (1 John 4:10).

"We love because he first loved us" (1 John 4:19).

That's the gospel. We either believe it or we don't. If we believe it, then we owe Him our life. That's why we surrender all to Him. Because the kingdom may come at a great price, but it's worth it.

"'You do not want to leave too, do you?' Jesus asked the Twelve. Simon Peter answered him, 'Lord, to whom shall we go? You have the words of eternal life'" (John 6:67-68).

Yes, kingdom living is hard. There is a price to living in the kingdom. But the greatest price is the one that Jesus paid so that we could have access to this kingdom. Jesus is the One who first prayed, "Not my will." He was the first to surrender His will, His way, His pride, His status, His comfort, His popularity.

He surrendered it all but gained freedom and access for you and me. The call today for you and me is to take a stand for the kingdom and not the culture. To be able to say like Peter, "Lord, you have the words of life. Where else would we go?"

WEEK 7

The Kingdom Rewards

“PETER SAID TO HIM, ‘WE HAVE LEFT EVERYTHING TO FOLLOW YOU.’”

MARK 10:28

7.1—LIFE, NOT DEATH

Well, as we begin our last week of Bible study, I pray that you are receiving all that God intends for you. I pray that as we studied the costs of the kingdom last week, that you have counted the costs and still decided to follow Jesus. This week we will look at the rewards of the kingdom, and friend, they are out of this world!

The first and most obvious reward of following Jesus is life—not just eternal life, but life right now as God intended for us to have.

Read again John 10:10. What did Jesus come to bring you?

Turn to Psalm 27. What is the one thing David asked of the Lord?

For David, the Lord's presence was only found in the tabernacle, but for you and me, His presence is wherever we are seeking Him. Look at verse 13 again.

Where did David say he would see the goodness of God?

That's right! Real life begins for us the moment we ask Jesus to be our Savior and Lord. His love, mercy, goodness, and faithfulness are with us now, in this life. Some of you may have been through traumatic experiences that seem to resemble death more than life. You may have a difficult time believing that God wants you to experience real life even now. If so, please read Jesus' Words here with me.

Read John 16:33. What does Jesus say we will have in this world?

Why does He say we can be encouraged?

Real life doesn't mean the absence of pain but the presence of Jesus.

My friend, that verse is really all we need to know. Real life doesn't mean the absence of pain, but the presence of Jesus. He is with us to walk through the difficulties of life and help us not only to survive but to thrive in the midst of pain. Following Jesus is hard! But navigating life without Him is much harder. He will give us the grace to endure whatever we go through.

Not only does the kingdom bring us life now, but we have the promise of life forever and an inheritance in the eternal kingdom.

Read the following verses and jot down a note about each one.

John 3:16

John 3:36

John 4:14

John 5:24

John 6:40

John 17:3

The kingdom of God leads to the kingdom of heaven; in fact, they are one and the same. When you follow Jesus into the kingdom of God, you become a citizen of heaven. This world is not our home. We are citizens of the kingdom of eternity where we will reign with Christ and inherit all that is His!

Philippians 3:20. Where is your citizenship?

You have an inheritance as a child of the kingdom.

Read these verses and take some notes on them.

Colossians 1:10-14

Colossians 3:23-24

Hebrews 9:15

1 Peter 1:3-5

2 Timothy 2:10-13

What does that inheritance look like?

Let's read a few more verses and take notes.

Matthew 25:19-23

Revelation 20:6

Romans 8:16-17

Sometimes we think of receiving the kingdom of God as "delayed gratification." We have to endure now so that we can receive later. Many think they would have to give up too much now just to receive a promise of something that may or may not come to pass. But for those who believe by faith that Jesus died to give us the kingdom right *now*, we have the joy of abundant life (even in the midst of pain) and the hope of an inheritance that will never fade.

Yes, we will have to give up a lot to live in the kingdom; but for everything we give up, Jesus repays us one hundred times more in eternity (Mark 10:29-31). On the contrary, if we do not live for the kingdom of God, we will not enter into the kingdom of heaven, but we will face an eternity in hell. That's the alternative.

Prayerfully fill in the chart below. Ask God to show you the rewards He has already blessed you with here in the "land of the living."

What I've given up to follow Jesus	What I've gained from following Jesus

7.2—PEACE, NOT CONFUSION

Honestly, I can think of so many rewards and blessings that come from following Christ, but I decided to choose the five that mean the most to me for this last week of study. Yesterday I chose life, because that is the one thing that every believer receives immediately upon choosing to follow Jesus. We are saved from hell and given an eternity (that's forever, folks!) to spend with God. If we never received another blessing from the Lord, that would be enough.

But God offers us so much more. Another incredible blessing of knowing the Lord is peace. Unless you have lived with the absence of peace, you can't fully appreciate the fullness of it. For those who have lived with inner turmoil, confusion, anxiety, stress, worry, fear, uncertainty, and strife, the promise of peace is sweet, indeed.

Read Psalm 29:11. Who is promised peace?

We are promised physical peace. Read Proverbs 14:30. What does a heart at peace give us?

We are promised mental peace. Read Isaiah 26:3. This peace affects what part of us?

We are promised emotional peace. Read John 14:27. What does this peace give us?

We are promised spiritual peace. Read Romans 5:1. What do you think "peace with God" means?

When we follow Jesus and enter the kingdom of God, we will have to turn away from some things of the world, but many of those things are what brought us the turmoil and confusion and strife in the first place. Surrendering our lives to the King brings us the settled state of a body free from anxiety (which can make us physically sick), a mind free from confusion, a heart free from bondage, and a spirit made right with God.

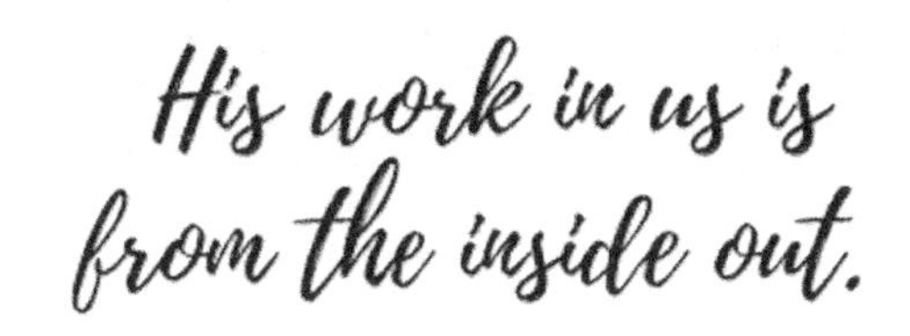

What God's Word doesn't promise is that we will be free from trouble or always at peace with man. His work in us is from the inside out. So our peace is an inner peace regardless of the world around us.

Read Matthew 10:34. What do you think this Scripture means?

Jesus is the Prince of Peace and He does promise us peace, but following Him sometimes creates conflict between the forces of darkness and the Light. This conflict may be seen in the world through war, terror, and evil. Because we belong to the kingdom of God, we will not always experience outward peace with the enemies of God. But with God we can rest in His inner peace, and we can work towards peace with others as much as is possible with us.

Read these Scriptures and take some notes:

Romans 12:18

Romans 14:19

1 Corinthians 7:15

How can you help to create peace in your circle of influence?

The promise of peace is demonstrated in our lives when we are able to live in a calm, stable, emotionally balanced way even in the midst of the enemy's chaos and confusion. For those of us who have been physically crushed by the weight of anxiety, mentally trapped by our fear and uncertainty, emotionally scarred by pain and confusion, and spiritually separated from God by our sin, the promise of peace is a soothing balm to our soul.

We may not always feel that peace within, but it is always available to us. All we have to do is remember His promises and sit at His feet. Worship will bring us back to a place of peace when prayer sometimes doesn't. No matter what we face, we have the promise of peace in the kingdom of God.

Isn't that worth every cost of following Jesus? It sure is to me.

Write a prayer below and tell the Father how thankful you are for His peace..

7.3—CONFIDENCE, NOT INSECURITY

One of the greatest blessings of following Jesus has been the confidence and security I have found in my relationship with Him. Let me see a show of hands. How many of you have struggled and/or still struggle with issues of insecurity? That's what I thought. Many past issues can cause us to feel insecure—having parents who divorced or abandoned us, bullying, peer pressure, and the list goes on. Our culture is constantly bombarding us with images and words that suggest we need to be more than what we are. But in Christ, we can be confident in who He created us to be.

First, we can believe by faith that God *is* our confidence. When we surrender our lives to the Lord, He makes us new from the inside out. The following Scripture was one of my favorites when I first got saved.

"I waited patiently for the Lord; he turned to me and heard my cry. He lifted me out of the slimy pit, out of the mud and mire; he set my feet on a rock and gave me a firm place to stand. He put a new song in my mouth, a hymn of praise to our God. Many will see and fear and put their trust in the Lord" (Psalm 40:1-3).

Insecurity makes us feel as if the rug will be pulled out from under us at any moment. We have no confidence. We are stuck in the miry clay of sin and insufficiency. But praise God, He lifts us out of that clay and gives us a firm place to stand, secure and confident in Him!

Read Proverbs 3:26. Who is our confidence?

Quite amazing, isn't it? Especially considering the fact that God is holy and we are sinners. And yet through Jesus, we can come into His presence with confidence and trust.

Read the following verses and jot down a few notes.

Ephesians 3:12

Hebrews 4:14-1

1 John 3:21-24

1 John 5:14

Second, we can feel confident in His love. I love that God gives us faith but He also allows us feelings. Sometimes, we just really need to feel His love for us. For me, the following verse changed my life as a college student coming to Christ for the first time. It was part of a blessing Moses spoke over the tribe of Benjamin, the youngest and least respected tribe. As a young girl abandoned by her father, I took these words to heart early in my walk with the Lord.

"Let the beloved of the Lord rest secure in him, for he shields him all day long, and the one the Lord loves rests between his shoulders" (Deuteronomy 33:12).

The image of riding on my Father's shoulders, secure in His love, was one that carried me through those early years. I may have given up the parties, the relationships, and the lies to follow Jesus; but I gained the security of a Father who loves me, and that was enough.

Read these verses and take some notes.

Psalm 16:5

Psalm 16:9

Hebrews 6:19

We have a confidence in which we can believe and a secure love which we can feel.

We have a confidence in which we can believe and a secure love which we can feel.

Third, we have a firm place that we can stand. When you live with insecurity, you don't feel as if you can stand on anything; but in the kingdom, we are on a firm foundation.

Read these Scriptures and jot down a few notes.

Psalm 37:23-24

Proverbs 10:25

2 Corinthians 1:21-24

1 Peter 5:10

I don't know about you, but the more of God's promises I read, the smaller those costs of the kingdom look. Despite what the world would have us believe, true confidence and security come from knowing and serving the Lord. Do you struggle with thoughts of comparison to others, not feeling good enough, or lacking in confidence? Journal your thoughts to the Lord today and ask Him to renew your mind with His truth.

7.4—JOY, NOT DESPAIR

Have you ever noticed how much despair is all around? Surely there is plenty to despair about: sickness, tragedy, war, and terror. The enemy has free reign over this world for now until Jesus returns. Because of the nature of sin, free will, and the devil, we do face many trials and griefs in this world. But one of the promises of the kingdom is joy.

Let's start today with something Jesus quoted from the Old Testament. In Luke 4:14-21 (you can turn there now), we see Jesus reading from the scroll of Isaiah in the synagogue.

What did Jesus tell His listeners in verse 21?

Now let's read all of this Scripture in Isaiah 61:1-7.

These are some of my very favorite Scriptures in all of the Bible. Jesus said that He was the fulfillment of this prophecy of Isaiah. Fill in the table below.

To those who are:	Jesus came to give:
Poor	
Brokenhearted	
Captive	
Prisoners	

Grieving	
Ashes	
Mourning	
Despairing	
Devastated	
Ruined	
Ashamed	
Disgraced	

This prophecy was spoken to the nation of Israel who had been taken captive in Babylon. The Lord through Isaiah was promising the coming of the Messiah Who would set the people free from sin. I believe this Scripture applied to them but also applies to all whom Jesus sets free from sin. The Gentiles (non-Jews) have been included in the promise of salvation. We do not replace the nation of Israel in Scripture. They are still the chosen nation to whom God has made many promises. But the promises of salvation, healing, and restoration above apply to all who call on the name of Jesus. He also promised joy and praise instead of despair. Let's look at some more Scriptures about this promise.

Read these verses and jot down some thoughts on each one.

John 15:9-11

Romans 14:17

Romans 15:13

James 1:2-3

1 Peter 1:8-9

The promises of joy are for those who have surrendered their lives to the Lord. We can't make our own rules and live by our own standard and expect to always have joy. And even when we do live surrendered to God, we will still face difficult circumstances. In the midst of those times, God will give us joy and peace. The key for us is to stay in His presence, in His Word, and in worship.

The key is for us to stay in His presence, in His Word, and in worship.

I remember when my daddy died. He had returned to us and become part of our lives after so many years away. With his loss, I felt such an intense sadness. I wanted to be able to touch him, to see him, to hug him, and sit on his lap, but I couldn't. The first Sunday after we buried him, I arrived at church to rehearse with the praise team. We circled up to pray, but I just began to weep. I just felt so sad. One of our praise team members told me I didn't have to sing and lead worship that day. They certainly understood my grief. But I wanted to sing.

I had planned the set list for worship a week in advance and all the slides were loaded into PowerPoint. We took to the stage and began to sing through the songs. And there it was—the song I had chosen the week before daddy died—"Trading My Sorrows." I don't know if you know the song, but it goes like this:

"I'm trading my sorrows. I'm trading my pain. I'm laying them down for the joy of the Lord."[xxii] No more appropriate words could have been on my tongue that day.

I opened my mouth and began to sing those words, trusting in the promise of my God, and joy flooded my soul. Peace reigned in my heart and the sadness was lifted, at least for the moment.

That, my friends, is the truth of God's promises. Sorrow will come; persecution will come. But the reward of walking in the kingdom is that at the feet of Jesus we can find joy in the midst of our greatest sorrow. And that's a reward of kingdom living that the world cannot give.

7.5—VICTORY, NOT DEFEAT

Life is a constant battle. We war against the flesh, the world, and the devil. Whether we decide to follow Jesus or not, we will still have to fight. That's why we have doctors, medicine, psychology, prisons, self-help books, exercise and diet regimens, anti-aging products. I could go on. In many nations, people battle just for food and clean water. They battle to survive against the elements or their enemies. Life is a constant battle.

The difference for those who know Jesus is that the battle has already been won.

The difference for those who know Jesus is that the battle has already been won. We don't grieve as those who have no hope. We don't fight without the promise of victory. Whether in this life or the next, we will have healing, restoration, deliverance, and perfect peace. We will experience the fountain of youth for all eternity. We will overcome death, hell, and the grave.

We will receive a victor's crown and the reward of the righteous. I don't know about you, but that trumps all that this world has to offer. Let's study some passages today.

Read Romans 8:18-39. What does Paul say will be revealed in us (v. 18)?

In verse 23, what does he say will be redeemed?

When we face trouble, hardship, persecution, famine, danger, nakedness, or sword, Paul says "in all these things we are ______________________."

Read these verses and jot down your thoughts.

1 Corinthians 15:50-58

2 Corinthians 2:14

1 John 5:1-5

In Christ, we have victory! Just as victors in a war take the spoils, we, too, will receive an inheritance and an eternal reward. Let's look at our inheritance, which is eternity with Jesus in the kingdom of heaven.

Read Colossians 1:10-14. Who receives this inheritance?

Read Colossians 3:23-24. Who gives this inheritance?

Read 1 Peter 1:3-5. Where is our inheritance kept?

If we have surrendered our lives to the Lordship of Jesus Christ, then one day we will receive our eternal inheritance, which is life forever in the presence of God. The Bible also teaches that we will be rewarded according to our works.

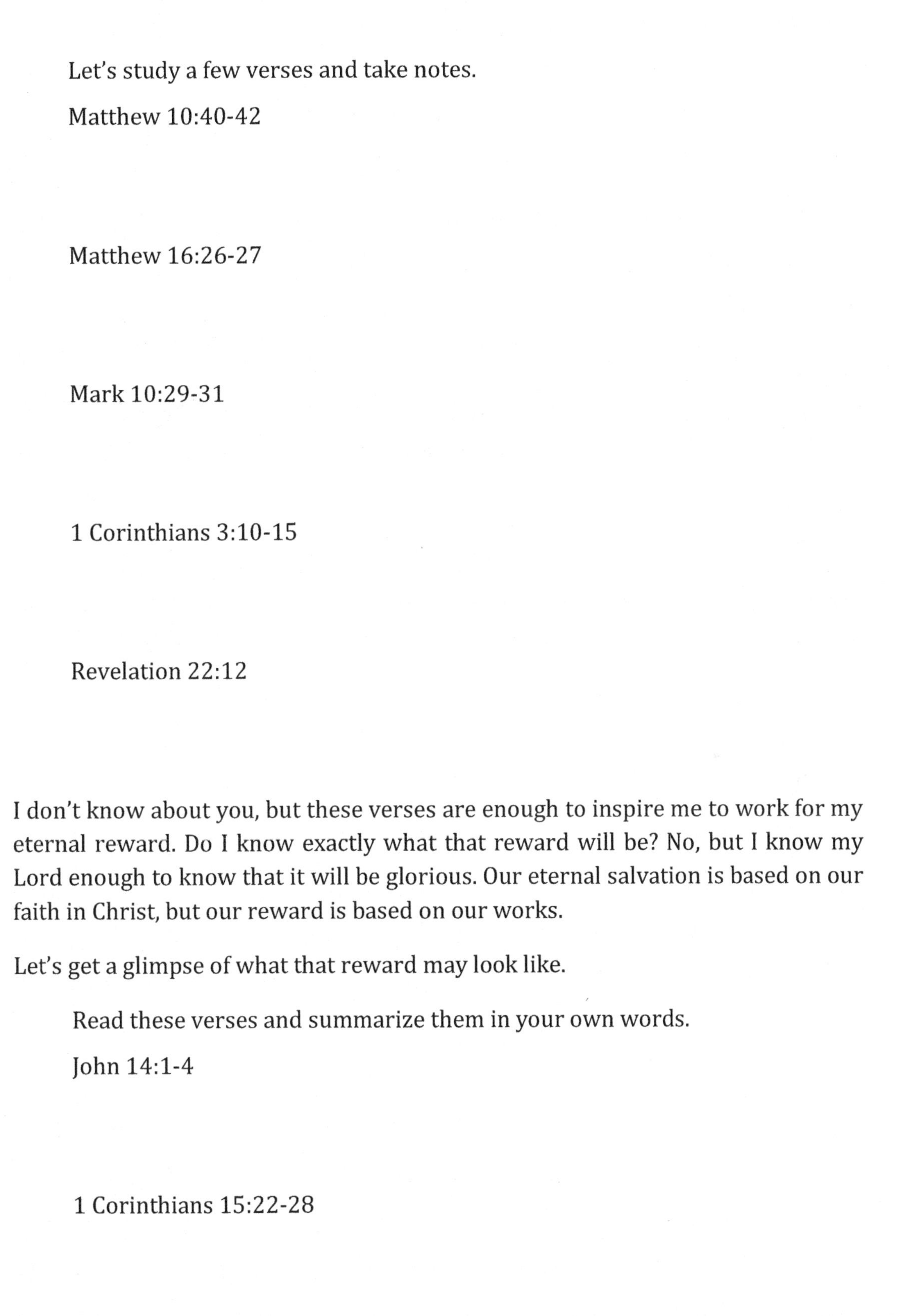

Let's study a few verses and take notes.

Matthew 10:40-42

Matthew 16:26-27

Mark 10:29-31

1 Corinthians 3:10-15

Revelation 22:12

I don't know about you, but these verses are enough to inspire me to work for my eternal reward. Do I know exactly what that reward will be? No, but I know my Lord enough to know that it will be glorious. Our eternal salvation is based on our faith in Christ, but our reward is based on our works.

Let's get a glimpse of what that reward may look like.

Read these verses and summarize them in your own words.

John 14:1-4

1 Corinthians 15:22-28

2 Timothy 2:11-12

Revelation 22:5

Jesus will reign and we will reign with Him. Every knee will bow and every tongue confess that He is Lord (Philippians 2:10-11). We will be there as those who have already bowed and surrendered to His Lordship. Hallelujah! We will reign with Him for a thousand years and then we will live forever in a place that He has prepared for us.

Our culture may think we are backwards, ignorant, or misinformed. The world may persecute and challenge our beliefs. But we will not shrink back and hide. We will shine for Jesus, the One Whom we have believed, knowing that our eternal reward far outweighs whatever we face on earth now. Faith is the victory!

WEEKEND DEVO:
THE KINGDOM REWARDS

I sit here with a lump in my throat as I write this last lesson for you. I have had you in my heart from Day 1. I so want you to know and understand that religion won't cut it. God seeks hearts who desire to know and follow Him. And our current climate is completely countercultural to all that Jesus taught.

On our last day together, I want to share a story with you from Acts 17:1-7. I'm using the King James Version because I want you to see a particular wording here.

> Now when they had passed through Amphipolis and Apollonia, they came to Thessalonica, where there was a synagogue of Jews: And Paul, as his manner was, went in unto them, and three Sabbath days reasoned with them out of the scriptures. Opening and alleging, that Christ must needs have suffered, and risen again from the dead; and that this Jesus, whom I preach unto you, is Christ. And some of them believed, and consorted with Paul and Silas; and of the devout Greeks a great multitude, and of the chief women not a few. But the Jews which believed not, took unto them certain lewd fellows of the baser sort, and gathered company, and set all the city on an uproar, and assaulted the house of Jason, and sought to bring them out to the people. And when they found them not, they drew Jason and certain brethren unto the rulers of the city, crying, "These that have turned the world upside down are come hither also; Whom Jason hath received: and these all do contrary to the decrees of Caesar, saying that there is another king, one Jesus" (KJV).

Did you get what Paul and those with him were accused of? Turning the world upside down. I don't know who was with Paul other than Silas, Timothy, and Luke. There could have been others, but regardless, there were not many, and yet they were accused of turning the world upside down! Do you know why? Simply for living the gospel. They didn't add to it, take away from it, or have a seeker-friendly service with a loud band and a light show. They simply preached the truth that Jesus was the Son of God who died and rose again for their salvation. And they were turning the world upside down.

Were they suffering persecution, prison, and riots? Yes. But many were coming to faith in Jesus and the Church was growing. When we truly love Jesus and share the truth of His kingdom, we will not be on a popular, easy path either.

We can't make Christianity fit our lifestyle. We can't try to cram Jesus into the mould we want Him to take so He fits nicely with our culture. We can't turn the church into a multi-million-dollar business or change the gospel presentation so that it appeals to those who are lost.

Because that's not who Jesus is.

We either surrender to him or reject Him, because He is Lord of all, and nothing I say or do can change that. Being a Jesus-follower is on His terms, not ours, and there is a cost. The question is—now that you know the costs, are you willing to still follow Him on His terms?

That was the question Jesus asked many of His followers, and we know that many of them turned back. Will you? Will you stay with Jesus when the going gets tough, when the persecution comes, when the dynamics of culture are uncertain?

Because, beloved, He stayed on course for you. Knowing the bloody torture and murder that He faced, Jesus walked through disappointment, rejection, betrayal, and denial to a rugged cross where He gave His life for you and me. Not because we were worthy, but because we were worth it.

The gospel message doesn't change. Jesus gave His life for you and me, so that if we believe in Him with all our hearts, we will have eternal life. We don't have to fix ourselves. We surrender to God and He changes us from the inside out. We don't have to try to build a kingdom on earth. We follow Jesus and He builds the kingdom through us. We don't have to convince others that Jesus is real. We live for Him and He shines through us. We don't have to make the gospel appealing to or relevant for today's culture. The gospel is appealing to those who recognize their need for a Savior, and it is relevant in every time and place.

For every need or excuse, Jesus is enough. He is the answer to every problem, the hope of every heart, and the deepest desire of the human condition.

You can join a church and still live for the world, but you will miss it. You can serve on committees, sing in the choir, and never sacrifice a thing for Jesus, but you will miss it. You can focus your life on yourself, your family, your career, your hobbies, your stuff, and your next vacation, but you will miss it.

You will miss what you were created for.

So, my question to you now is this: Do you want religion or do you want a relationship with the Creator of the universe? Relationship requires sacrifice. It comes with a cost. But it also comes with great reward.

My prayer is that you will choose to surrender your entire life to the Lord of Life, no matter the cost. The harvest is great. The workers are few. Will you dare to be a woman who seeks worship, who loves the Word, and who takes it to her world for the sake of Jesus?

That, my friends, is what it's really all about—allowing Jesus Christ to turn your life inside out and letting Him use you to turn the world upside down.

Because intimacy with Jesus truly does change *everything*.

How to Have New Life

Do you want to know how to have new life?

We were each created by God to know and worship Him. God loves you and desires a personal relationship with you.

The Bible teaches us that we are all sinners. Romans 3:23 says, "for all have sinned and fall short of the glory of God." God is holy and righteous and good. He created the world and all that is in it. But we are all born with a sinful nature because He made us with a free will—the opportunity to choose whether or not we will follow Him. Left to ourselves, we will fall short of His glory and righteousness. This sin separates us from God and leads only to death. Romans 6:23 says, "for the wages of sin is death."

But because God loves us so much, He made a way for us to know Him through His Son. "But God demonstrates his own love for us in this: while we were still sinners, Christ died for us" (Romans 5:8). God sent His only Son, Jesus, who lived a perfect life, to die on the cross for us as payment for our sin. He took the punishment on Himself so that we could be free from sin's penalty.

The rest of Romans 6:23 (above) says this: "but the gift of God is eternal life in Christ Jesus." We are sinners, and yet through Jesus and the gift of God, we can have eternal life. The truth is that we really can have a personal relationship with God through His Son, Jesus.

So what do you do to be saved?

Romans 10:9-10 tells us "That if you confess with your mouth, 'Jesus is Lord,' and believe in your heart that God raised him from the dead, you will be saved. For it is with your heart that you believe and are justified, and it is with your mouth that you confess and are saved."

If God is speaking to your heart right now and you want to be saved, pray a prayer like this one:

> *Lord God,*
>
> *I believe that You are God and that You created me to know You. I believe that You sent your Son to die on the cross for my sins and that He rose again and lives forever. I know that I am a sinner and I confess my sins to You now. I ask You to forgive me and cleanse me and come to live inside my heart and be the Lord of my life. I choose to follow You and live for You from this day forward.*
>
> *In Jesus' name,*
>
> *Amen*

If you just prayed a prayer like this one, please let me know the good news. You can contact me at deuter3312@gmail.com. Find a Bible-believing Christian church and begin to read the Bible and talk to God every day. You've just begun your new life in Him. Congratulations! Your life will never be the same!

Small Group and One-on-One Ideas

This study works great with a group, with a partner, or alone with the Lord. If you are meeting one-on-one, here are some suggestions for your time together:

- Meet at least once a week to discuss the lessons and go over your answers to the questions.
- Begin each meeting with prayer.
- Don't be afraid to share your questions, doubts, or concerns with one another; that's the whole point of accountability and mentorship.
- Be committed to completing the work each week and to your partner.
- Share any revelation God gives you and encouragement you received during the week with each other.
- Challenge each other to live out the lessons you are learning.

If you are meeting in a small group, try these ideas:

- All of the above suggestions still apply.
- Remember that each of you in the group will be at different places spiritually. Give others room to grow and share without judgment.
- Have a time-keeper who keeps the discussion moving forward so the meetings don't go too long.
- Don't be afraid to stop and pray for a sister if she is struggling.
- Support each other throughout the week through texts and calls.
- Set up a group on Messenger to keep up with prayer requests, cancellations, etc.

- Enjoy a meal together each week to encourage fellowship and unity.
- When you finish the study, consider a meal out or spiritual retreat to celebrate, recap what you have learned, and continue to grow in fellowship and unity with one another.

Please share photos of your study time on social media with the hashtag #insideoutbiblestudy so we can all share the fun together!

Acknowledgments

I would like to thank those in my life who made this work possible. To my very first pastor and his wife, Jody and Michelle Flowers, thank you for investing in me. Your example of discipleship is still the standard in my book. Love you both!

Once again, this was a Bible study written originally for my students at Jesus Is Lord Christian School. To Pastor Allen and "Miss" Glenda, all of the school staff, students, and parents, thank you for twelve years of teaching at the best job ever. I'll never forget all that you have taught me.

To Pastor Blake, Bridgette and my church family at Salem Baptist Church, thank you for the prayers, support, encouragement, and lessons that enabled me to grow and learn how to do church well.

Thank you, Mema and all the ladies of my Thursday night Bible study. Without your correction, encouragement, and prayers, I wouldn't be the woman I am today.

To Kenneth, Josiah, Moriah, and Bethany, your love means more to me than anything in this world. Thank you for loving me even when I am unlovable. Thank you for giving me the space and the inspiration to write.

And to my Jesus, You are the name above every name, the Love of my life, and the reason for everything that I do. I pray this work brings you glory.

About the Author

Jennifer Hayes Yates is a wife, mom, and empty-nester who enjoys reading, writing, and drinking coffee, especially while hanging out with friends. Having taught in Christian education for twenty-two years, she has a passion for communicating God's truth and inspiring others to follow Him.

Jennifer now writes a weekly blog, is active on social media, and is working on her fourth book. She serves in her church as a Sunday school teacher and music director and leads a small group of awesome ladies in Bible study at her home.

She's the best-selling author of *Seek Him First: How to Hear from God, Walk in His Will, and Change Your World* and *Let's Run! Running the Race with Faith and Perseverance*, a 6-week Bible study, but she's still just seeking to glorify God in all she writes and make a few disciples along the way.

You can keep up with Jennifer on Facebook, Instagram, and at jenniferhyates.com.

Note from the Author

Thank you so much for taking the time to read this book. I so pray that you have been blessed and that you have grown in your relationship with the Lord and your desire to be on mission with Him.

I really value your feedback and would love to hear what you think. Please consider leaving a helpful review on Amazon. Your reviews help Amazon put this book in the hands of more people, and they give me the tools to make the next book better!

Thanks so much!

Jen

SELF-PUBLISHING
SCHOOL

End Notes

[i] Merriam-Webster's Learner's Dictionary (online).

[ii] Kenneth Barker, The NIV Study Bible (Grand Rapids, MI: Zondervan, 1984), 1445.

[iii] Chaim Bentorah, *Biblical Hebrew Studies* (online) available at http://www.chaimbentorah.com/2013/01/devotional-matthew-1916-17/.

[iv] Translated by J.G. Pilkington. From Nicene and Post-Nicene Fathers, First Series, Vol. 1. Edited by Philip Schaff. (Buffalo, NY: Christian Literature Publishing Co., 1887.) Revised and edited for New Advent by Kevin Knight. http://www.newadvent.org/fathers/110101.htm

[v] Becky Tirabassi, *Sacred Obsession* (Carol Stream, Illinois: Tyndale, 2006), 7.

[vi] Henrietta C. Mears, *What the Bible Is All About* (Ventura, California: Regal Books, 1953, revised 1997), 217.

[vii] Ibid., 208.

[viii] Mike Bickle, "Session 4 An Overview of the Storyline of the Song of Songs," from the Online Teaching Library at www.mikebickle.org, 2007.

[ix] Mike Bickle, "Session 3 The Divine Kiss: Transformed by the Word," from the Online Teaching Library at www.mikebickle.org, 2007.

[x] Mike Bickle, "Session 9 Dark in the Heart, But Lovely to God," from the Online Teaching Library at www.mikebickle.org.

[xi] Barker, 1871.

[xii] Ibid., 1787.

[xiii] Mike Bickle, "Session 10 Her Journey Begins with Spiritual Crisis," from the Online Teaching Library at www.mikebickle.org.

[xiv] Ibid.

[xv] https://www.thattheworldmayknow.com/religious-movements-of-jesus-time

[xvi] Mears, 698.

[xvii] John R. Kohlenberger, Ed., *NIV Exhaustive Bible Concordance*, Third Edition (Grand Rapids: Zondervan, 1990, 1999, 2015), 1562.

[xviii] Barker, 1449.

[xix] Kohlenberger, 1554.

[xx] "Opportunity Cost," *Investopedia* available online at www.investopedia.com.

[xxi] Kohlenberger, 1439.

[xxii] Darrell Evans, "Trading My Sorrows," *Freedom* (Vertical Music, 1998).

SHLUFZYMSVZWDQ

Made in the USA
Columbia, SC
17 August 2021